ANGLESEY
NATUREWATCH

PHILIP SNOW

AMBERLEY

This edition first published 2021

Amberley Publishing
The Hill, Stroud
Gloucestershire GL5 4EP

www.amberley-books.com

British Library Cataloguing in Publication Data.
A catalogue record for this book is available from the British Library.

ISBN 978 1 3981 0480 8 (print)
ISBN 978 1 3981 0481 5 (ebook)

Typesetting by SJmagic DESIGN SERVICES, India.
Printed in Great Britain.

CONTENTS

YNYS BADRAIG
WYLFA HEAD
THE SKERRIES
CEMLYN LAGOON
MAEN Y BUGAIL
Cemaes Bay
Tregele
Llanfairynghornwy
Mynydd
Mechell
Church Bay
CARREGLWYD
Llanfaethlu
LLYN ALAV
Llanddeusant
Llynnon Mill
Llanfwrog
BREAKWATER COUNTRY PARK
Holyhead/Port
Llanfachraeth
SOUTH STACK
ALAW
ESTUARY
LLYN LLYWENAN
PENRHOS
BEDDMANARCH
BAY
Bodedern
Valley
THE RANGE
INLAND SEA
Trearddur
Bay
Caergeiliog
PORTH DIANA
Bryngwran
VALLEY WETLANDS
Gwalchma
Rhoscolyn
LLYN MAELOG
YNYS
FEIRIG
Rhosneigr
LLYN
CORON
Beth
ABERFFRAW
COMMON
Aberffraw
Hermon
COB PO
CEFNI
ESTUAR
Bodorgan
NEWBOR
FOREST
YNYS LLANDL

VEN
BULL BAY
YNYS AMLWCH
POINT LYNAS
Amlwch
Llaneilian
Penysarn
DULAS ESTUARY
sgoch
PARYS MOUNTAIN
LLIGWY
Rhosybol
Brynrefail
Moelfre
rchymedd
BODAFON MOUNTAIN
CORS
ERDDREINIOG
Benllech
FEDW FAWR
PUFFIN ISLE
RED WHARF BAY
MARIANDYRYS
PENMON
CORS GOCH
Llanddona
Pentraeth
LLANGOED
COMMON
CORS BODEILIO
CEFNI RESERVOIR
PENTRAETH FOREST
ABERLLEINIOG
HENLLYS
THE DINGLE - NANT Y PANDY
Llansadwrn
Beaumaris
Llangefni
CYTIR MAWR
MENAI STRAIT
angristiolus
CAEAU PEN Y CLIP
THE SPINNIES
'CORS DDYGA
Menai Bridge
MALLTRAETH
Penrhyn
MARSH
Gaerwen
Llanfair PG
Castle
RSPB
COED CYRNOL
Bangor
AFON
CEFNI
Llanddaniel Fab
PLAS NEWYDD
aeth
Llangaffo
COED
YN PARC
Brynsiencyn
PORTHAMEL
AWR
Newborough
Dwyran
FOEL FERRY
BOROUGH
Caernarfon
REN
BRAINT ESTUARY
FORYD BAY

FOREWORD BY IOLO WILLIAMS

Anglesey, or Ynys Môn, has always been blessed with a wide mosaic of habitats that support a mouth-watering variety of wildlife. Indeed, some of my earliest memories include visiting the island with my late grandfather in the 1960s and watching lapwing and curlew chicks on the mosaic of small, damp meadows.

Anglesey also has a long history of excellent naturalists and artists, dedicated individuals that have worked diligently to record the island's feast of wildlife. Philip Snow has earned his place among this elite group and this, his latest book, is one of his best.

Never before has Anglesey had every wildlife nook and cranny documented quite like this. From choughs and terns to silver-studded blue butterflies, red squirrels and spatulate fleawort, all the island's notable wildlife makes an appearance as Philip combines his encyclopaedic wildlife knowledge with his undoubted ability as an artist.

In all, fifty of Anglesey's best wildlife sites are included in this book, giving comprehensive coverage of habitats and species, and an excellent geographical spread. Whether you are a resident or a visitor, this book is perfect for all your island wildlife needs and it will undoubtedly be an invaluable addition to anyone's library. I urge you to buy it, use it, enjoy Anglesey's wildlife and help conserve it for future generations.

Introducing Anglesey

This glorious island – known by several names throughout its long history including Ynys Mona, 'Isle of Apples-Affalon', Anglesey, and now, once again, Ynys Môn – is enjoying a bit of a renaissance in its wildlife, even though it has recently lost several key species. The likes of corncrake, red helleborine orchid and natterjack toad might have gone, but several others are moving in. Among them are an amazing three species of Mediterranean egret, red kites, uncommon insects and fungi, while others, like red squirrel, otter and bittern, are rapidly returning, with and without our help. Our superb rocky and sandy coastline also shows both loss and gain. Auks including Atlantic puffin, some terns and cetaceans like porpoises and dolphins are increasing, while other species such as breeding shelduck or Atlantic salmon are in decline. Generally though, the biggest losses are formerly common but long-declining breeding birds like skylark, lapwing, redshank, grey partridge, yellowhammer, curlew, cuckoo, greenfinch, green woodpecker and little owl. Yet we also have windblown southern insects like hummingbird hawkmoth and clouded yellow butterfly increasing, or red fox, badger, polecat and common buzzard, which have seen their numbers shoot up in recent decades. Such complexity! This is mainly symptomatic of specific changes in farming and general 'tidying up' practices, as well as climate.

Fortunately, we still have a wonderful range of habitats for all our wildlife: cliffs, islands, stacks and coves, harbours and 'inland sea', coast maritime heaths, saline lagoons, sand dunes, estuaries and the Menai Strait, dry inland heaths, assorted farmlands, hedgerows, 'green lanes', meadows, lakes, pools, small rivers, marshes and fens and even woods and forests – and a wonderful coast path. Yet we also need lots of people and organisations to help preserve Anglesey's wildlife and scenery, and if possible, restore lost species or habitats. Predictably, this is mainly done through the protection and management of places vital for particular wildlife – the bittern's return is largely thanks to restoring its essential reed bed habitat at RSPB's Malltraeth Marsh or NRW's Cors Erddreiniog, and protecting South Stack and the Skerries for many breeding terns, auks and Atlantic puffins – but such places are important for a whole range of flora and fauna (F&F).

In fact, virtually all our wildlife is liable to change in status – whether caused by us, environment or climate – from reptiles to amphibians, insects to flowers and fungi, or fish, seals and other charismatic marine life like cetaceans (dolphins, etc.). Yet it's not all due to us or climatic warming, for the likes of breeding fulmar, petrel, eider duck and skuas have only recently arrived in Britain from the cold north, and Cetti's warbler, glossy ibis and purple heron increasingly arrive from the warm European south. Then there's little and cattle egret that have only recently colonised Britain from Europe, but are already leap-frogging all the way over to America. Unfortunately, some new species are not so welcome, like grey squirrel, 'escapee' mink, or the accidentally introduced and invasive Japanese knotweed, Himalayan balsam or Oxford ragwort!

Yet an increase in mammals like polecat, stoat, red squirrel and otter is often down to us – as either deliberate reintroduction (red squirrels) or easing of persecution and cleaning up of the environment (otter). Rabbits paint a more complex picture, for when this Roman introduction is plentiful, so will its predators be, from common buzzards to mustelid species like stoat. As for hedgehogs, we don't really know why they are in decline, apart from farm/garden chemicals or roadkill.

Other species remain more or less stable here as long as there is enough watery habitat or 'rough' ground – hence good numbers of reptiles and amphibians like slow-worm, adder, common frog and common toad. Newts, too, like the rare great crested, smooth (common) and lots of palmate, or lizards, mainly the common, and even the recently reintroduced and bright green sand lizard, if still rare and localised. One of the biggest changes relates to seabirds like terns, which used to breed on our coasts but the sheer amount of human activity has largely restricted them to a few especially protected isles. Another important phenomena, wintering

Red squirrel, Newborough.

wildfowl and wader flocks, if sometimes declining are still plentiful in the case of green and golden plover, or even occasionally increasing, like brent geese.

One of the biggest losses is undoubtedly farmland birds (and related insects, flowers and small mammals), as changing practices often mean big transformation. Added to the pressure of more people than ever using the environment, let alone omnipresent 'climate change', Anglesey has probably changed more in the last fifty years than since the great island-splitting wetland of Malltraeth Marsh was drained, and the Cob embankment built, in 1817. That was done to both reclaim farming land and for coal mining at Pentre Berw (now an Industrial Heritage site and RSPB reserve), carrying on Anglesey's long history of land use. It also demonstrates how brownfield industrial sites can be good for wildlife – often better than the barren ryegrass 'green' fields developed for stock animals. Then there are places like the Iron Age hill fort at Bwrdd Arthur, now an attractive nature reserve, its long history buried under swathes of limestone-loving plants and spiralling skylarks. Alternately, the toxic mining legacy of Amlwch's famous 'Copper Mountain' means few plants can survive, not that gyring ravens, hunting barn owls, bright stonechats or roosting gulls are badly affected. So often the island's long history, from iconic stone monuments to once busy harbours, lighthouses, lime and brick kilns, or flooded peat and coal diggings, are also good for wildlife. Holyhead's South Stack and Breakwater Park, Porth Llanlleiana and Porth Wen (Sites 2 and 42) are all good examples. As is Anglesey's world-famous geology, the original source of our magnificent cliffs and isles. (More information from Oriel Môn or Geo-Môn in Amlwch Port).

Whether mining, farming, fishing or forestry, and now sun, wind and even wave 'farming', we have and are still affecting the natural world – for good or ill. Yet we have always cleared much of the woodland and scrub to make way for agriculture and settlement, both losing and gaining a whole variety of F&F. Anglesey was aptly named 'Môn Mam Cymru', the 'Mother'/'Breadbasket of Wales' in medieval times, for its important grain and apple crops, and the loss of them also meant the loss of many birds, mammals, flowers and insects. Even their protective surrounds,

Chough and peregrine, South Stack Lighthouse.

the field headlands and edges, stone walls and hedgerow habitats, all held a wide variety of interactive F&F. Drystone walls host a wealth of life from stoats to common lizards, insects to lichens and mosses. Yet when sheep and cattle replaced crops, other wildlife augmented our countryside – until it became too intensive and/or agri-chemicalised, or fields and marshes were drained (although not as badly as other parts of Britain, where mass removal of hedgerows and over use of chemicals has sometimes wreaked 'ecocide').

The aforementioned farm birds, brown hare and the likes of small mammals such as field mice suffer from the lack of winter fallow fields and 'weed' seeds, or are simply the victims of too-early cutting of silage. Or those waders like lapwing and curlew, once common breeders in our countryside, which now usually breed only in damp and 'unkempt' reserves like RSPB Malltraeth Marsh. There grazing is strictly managed for the good of a wide variety of plants, hence most wildlife, especially birds – but also because miles of electric fences keep red foxes out!

Bittern & Marsh Harrier

Bittern and marsh harrier.

A modest sustainable farming approach can also be seen in new solar farm, where sheep or crops can be sustained among the large fields of solar panels. Not quite biodiversity or rewilding, the current buzz-words, but we need to compromise on environmental issues like this. Yet, the main reason for Anglesey's current success in conservation is more down to specially maintained or created reserves – although the new potato, hemp or corn crops can also shelter the likes of grey partridge and other F&F. We are also successfully recreating habitats, especially marsh and wetland habitats, which have their very wide range of plants and related F&F. That includes the lovely pink flowering rush; various dragonflies like the broad-bodied chaser and southern hawker; butterflies like the marsh fritillary; mammals like otters, water and field voles; or kingfishers, marsh harriers, reed warblers and the famous bittern, all of which are enjoying a renewed lease of life on Môn. All can be seen at wetlands like Cors Ddyga, flourishing alongside the busy cycle track and web of footpaths around the Afon Cefni.

Paths, especially our long Coast Path, are essential for seeing sites as different as South Stack or Newborough Forest, famed either for seabirds or the emblematic red squirrel. Both also regularly feature on national TV. Little wonder with our glorious scenery, changeable sea light and dramatic weather! We also have the warm Gulf Stream, Atlantic low-pressure systems, European heat and cold, and the shapely hills of Snowdonia/Eryri and the Llŷn Peninsula overlooking and influencing us. Added to the ebb and flow of twice-daily tides, it ensures this island always has somewhere suitable for many activities. Long known for beaches and water sports, there are always wilder places to explore, or indoor attractions associated with nature, like the Sea Zoo, Oriel Môn, Llynon Mill or Moelfre's Sea-Life Centre. Few places are as compact and varied as Môn!

Note also the art of C. F. Tunnicliffe and Kyffin Williams, both RA and OBE, both great expositors of Anglesey's unique landscape and wildlife and celebrated in Oriel Môn and many publications.

Oystercatchers, Puffin Isle.

50 ANGLESEY NATURE SITES

SITE 1: SOUTH STACK AND THE RANGE
OS reference SH 205-823

South Stack is deservedly one of Anglesey's most famous beauty, as well as birding, spots, with its spectacular lighthouse island and soaring cliffs – and RSPB Bird Observatory, Shop and Café (A). One of the main attractions here are the thousands of cliff-nesting auks like guillemots and razorbills, or kittiwake, fulmar petrel and gull species, as well as resident peregrine falcon, common raven and (red-billed) chough. Most of the action can be seen in comparative comfort from Ellin's Tower observatory (B), which has wheelchair access from the RSPB members car park (C) There's also the Anglesey Coast Path (ACP) and a whole network of tracks to choose from, in both Holyhead and Trearddur Bay directions.

One of the other attractions is the cliff maritime heath itself, especially grazed for the choughs, uncommon silver-studded blue butterfly or rare plants like the endemic spathulate fleawort, spotted rock rose, red form of kidney vetch and wild carrot. Metallic green tiger beetles, rose chafers, and black and scarlet six spot burnet moth are also found here among the many other insects. Reptiles like common lizard and adder like the rocks, tufted grasses, heathers and gorses, while bright birds like stonechat and linnet use them for prominent perches, or the meadow and rock pipits that overlap here. The cliffs are especially attractive in early summer when swathes of pink, blue and white flowering sea thrift, spring squill and sea campion are on show.

South Stack is also handy for accessing the great views from Holyhead Mountain, North Stack Lighthouse, or archaeological sites like Ty Mawr and Cytaiu'r Gwyddelod ('Irishman's Hut Circles') (D). The more adventurous can descend the steep switchback of 390 stone steps to the lighthouse island itself (tickets from RSPB Café/Shop), where the three most common gull species – herring, greater and lesser black-backed, and great cormorant and shag – breed, and Atlantic puffin can usually be found. The 'sea parrots' can also be observed on the sea, by the tower, and may even be on live video, like the regular chough and auk nests. The tower is also full of (my!) interpretation panels of the F&F, helpful wardens and telescopes. The café and picnic area is also a good place to see choughs, or nearby fields, where a wide range of birds, including spring ring ouzels and wheatears, and autumn's large numbers of hirundines (swallows, etc.), finches and thrushes pass over.

An impressive number of rare birds have been seen here, from black-browed albatross, Russian black lark and American catbird to more familiar Eurasian ones

SITE 1 - SOUTH STACK & THE RANGE

Peregrine
Puffin

SOUTH
STACK

Razorbills &
Guillemots

Grey Seal & pup

Holyhead
Mountain

→ Holyhead

Anglesey Coast path

Footpaths-Tracks

[A] [D]

[B]

[C]

[F]

Rosechafer

Spotted
Rockrose

Silver-studded
Blue

Spathulate
Fleawort

[E]
THE RANGE

Porth
Dafarch

Trearddur
Bay →

(Red-billed) Choughs

like hobby, red-rumped swallow, bluethroat, bee-eater, wryneck or uncommon shrikes and warblers. Then virtually any north-west-facing headland around here can attract such birds, particularly at migration time (see the Cambrian Ornithological Society yearly report or check the web).

This is also a great place to look down on frolicking cetaceans, like common and bottle-nosed dolphins, or the massive and pale Risso's dolphin, and especially smaller harbour porpoises. You may even see minke whales (7–8 metres), and, rarely, killer whales, although you are much more likely to see the decidedly friendlier-looking grey seal around the rocks – keep an eye out for their creamy

Manx shearwaters.

pups from September onwards, on virtually any rocky coast. More wonder: the reappearance of shoals of large blue-fin tuna! Probably the return of good numbers of their prey, like herring and mackerel, is responsible, themselves dependent on huge numbers of large zooplankton called copepods, which are increasingly coming north.

Manx shearwater and northern gannet are the commonest sea passage birds here, especially after autumn storms drive them into Liverpool Bay. This is often the best time to see them returning westwards, and a whole slew of other possible pelagic (deep sea) birds, like divers, terns, skuas, petrels, grebes, or sea duck like common scoter, eider and long-tailed duck (for a fuller 'pelagic' list see Site 37: Lynas Point).

The nearby Range (coast defence during the Second World War) (E) has many of the same birds as South Stack on its rolling maritime heath or spectacular coves and cliffs. One of its specialities is the elusive but amazingly tame dotterel, normally a northern mountain bird but one that briefly rests en route on several headlands or hills here. Rare Balearic and sooty shearwaters have been spotted among the many passing seabirds, while merlins often hunt the small passerines (and short-eared owls the mammals) from autumn to spring. The hooded crows around here are often the darker 'crosses' with resident carrion crows, as vagrant hoodies have much lighter grey trimmings.

Note two little reservoirs (F) on the Holyhead road, which are often worth checking for unusual terns like white-winged black or whiskered tern and even an American killdeer plover. Other regular birds for the area include kestrel, oystercatcher, skylark, pied wagtail, raven and jackdaw, and in summer one might see whimbrel, swallow, house and sand martin, swift, cuckoo, whitethroat, whinchat, common, Arctic, sandwich and black terns, Arctic, great, long-tailed and pomarine skua, and storm and Leach's petrel. In winter black redstart can be spotted.

RSPB, South Stack Trust, CADW, ACP, Gwynedd Archaeological Trust

SITE 2: BREAKWATER COUNTRY PARK AND HOLYHEAD HARBOUR
OS reference SH 215-835

Just north-west of the busy town and Irish ferry port, Ynys Môn Breakwater Country Park nestles in an old quarry and brickworks, and is now an attractive visitor centre (A). It's a great example of industrial archaeology and wildlife side-by-side, with access to cliff, coast and heathland F&F, and by the ACP and North Stack lighthouse headland (B). It also has an information centre, café, NWWT

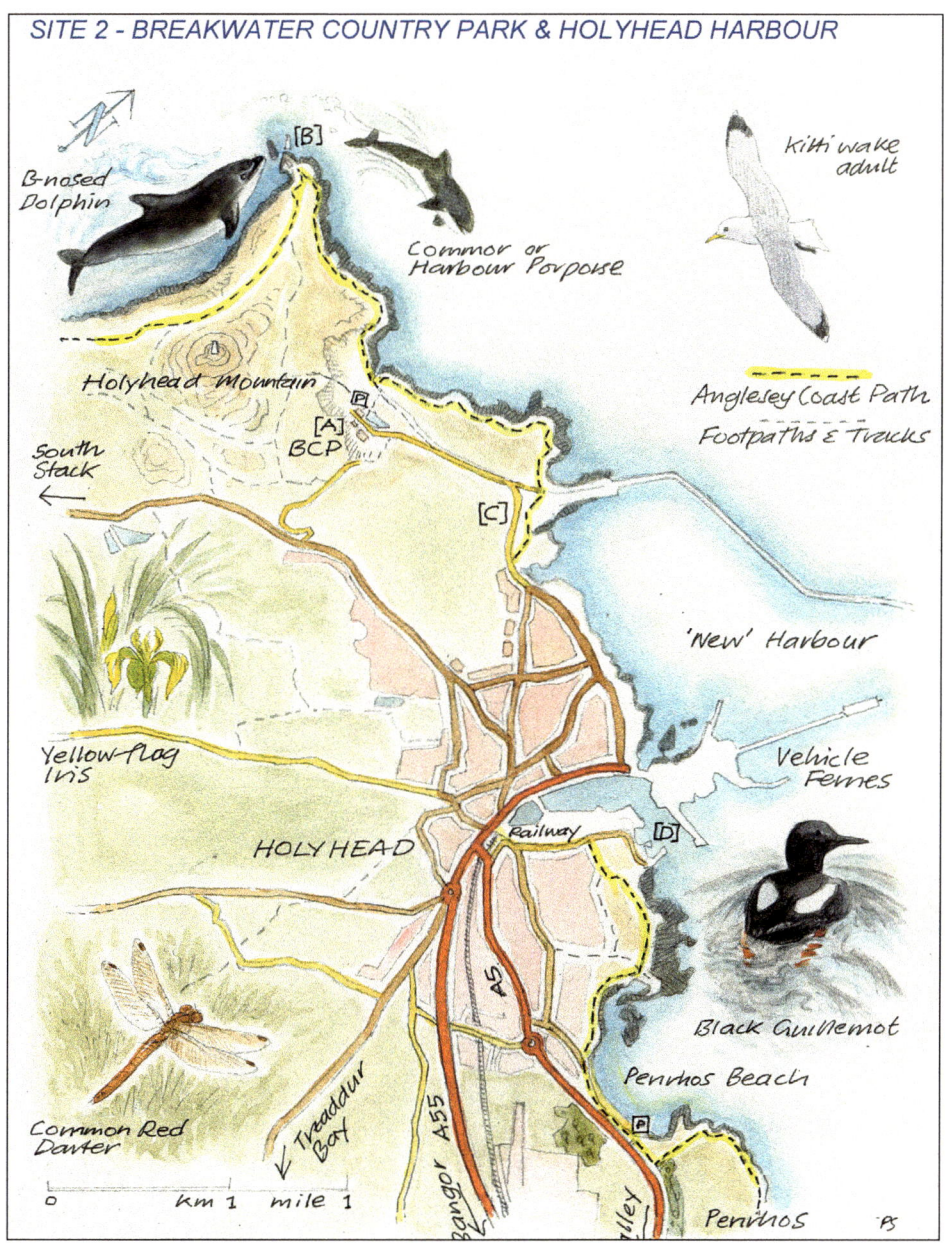

SITE 2 - BREAKWATER COUNTRY PARK & HOLYHEAD HARBOUR

B-nosed Dolphin
[B]
Common or Harbour Porpoise
Kittiwake adult
Holyhead Mountain
[A] BCP
South Stack
Anglesey Coast Path
Footpaths & Tracks
[C]
'New' Harbour
Yellow-flag Iris
Vehicle Ferries
HOLYHEAD
Railway
[D]
Black Guillemot
Penrhos Beach
Common Red Darter
Treaddur Bay
Bangor A55
Penrhos
km 1   mile 1

shop, fishing pool and outdoor art gallery. The distinctive brick, beehive kilns building is roofless, so prints of Tunnicliffe, the Massey sisters flowers and this author's work are printed on metal, alongside archaeological and maritime history. There's also my panel for the pool's wildlife, Llyn Llwynog and Pwll Ffynnon. They commonly host mallard, 'mere-hen' (moorhen) and grey heron, in addition to many dragonflies and damselflies like the red darter or common blue damselfly. The lake is stocked with 'coarse' fish like carp and roach. It's only a short walk to the nearby grey seal breeding coves (autumn) and regular harbour porpoise sightings, or to a whole network of far easier, flatter tracks than the steep climb up to the wild North Stack headland, lighthouse and impressive caves. The rocky heath, quarries, meadows and wetlands also ensure reptiles, such as adder, slow-worm and common lizard, and amphibians, such as common frogs and toads, as well as the usual palmate, and probably even great-crested newts – Môn is a bit of a haven for this rarity.

The birds are headed by the 'big three' cliff denizens: peregrine falcon, common raven and red-billed chough. Little owls too, if often hard to see among the rocks, while bright orange-fronted stonechats (male) are more prominent as they irately 'chack' from the top of ling, bell or cross-leaved heathers, western gorse or bracken. The coast is often dominated by noisy oystercatchers, as well as a few turnstone or purple sandpipers in winter. Typically gulls and the likes of auks and kittiwakes (mainly in summer) can be seen with great cormorant and shag, as well as passerines like rock and meadow pipits, linnet, goldfinch, and summer wheatear. Curlew and whimbrel also regularly rest on the rocks. Energetic flocks of jackdaws can typically be seen swirling about the cliffs, while other corvids

Great crested newt.

like carrion crow, rook and magpie are also common, as are rock/feral pigeons. With so many bushes, hedges and small trees, summer warblers like willow, garden, chiffchaff and whitethroat join one of our most beautiful, if elusive, species – bullfinch – among the other usual finches, tits and other common garden/ woodland birds. The area is also an SSSI (Site of Special Scientific Interest) for other F&F like the beautiful bee orchid, or many moths and butterflies like the small copper, gatekeeper, common and the rare silver-studded blue (as on South Stack, or Llandudno's Great Ome).

Mammals are also quite well represented, with badgers regularly among the usual red fox, stoat, weasel, hedgehog, mole and smaller voles, mice and shrews, and even a rare Irish bat has been found among commoner species like pipistrelle and brown long-eared bat. Doubtless polecat and increasing numbers of otters, too, as well as, unfortunately, the odd stinky American mink (mink scats stink, otter's fishy spraints are pleasantly fishy!).

Note the important – if somewhat untidy – birdwatching site of Soldiers Point (C). The scruffy little lane that runs past the ruined government building out to Soldiers Point and its small cove has turned up many a good bird, especially in spring and autumn. The hedgerows and bushes are especially attractive to autumn passage birds like the smart little yellow-browed warbler and firecrest, among regular flocks of tits and goldcrest, usually including long-tailed tit. Winter redwing and fieldfare flocks also occur, as do woodcock, snipe, water rail, and lapwing on the damp fields nearby. The small cove has the usual coast birds, whilst little holes in the long breakwater host breeding black guillemots.

The busy harbour often shelters winter great northern and black-throated diver, or Slavonian grebe, and other sea fowl from the frequent storms. Nowadays, kingfishers are seen here and in the Old Harbour (D), which is also good for black guillemot and one or two wintering glaucous gulls – if no more than the one massive white-billed diver that entertained us back in 1991!

ACP, Anglesey County Council, AONB, NWWT

SITE 3: PORTH DIANA, TREARDDUR BAY AND RHOSCOLYN COAST
OS reference SH 254-782

Porth Diana (A) is a little yachting cove adjacent to Trearddur Bay that hides a tiny heathland reserve behind it, noted for rare spotted rock-rose – Anglesey's adopted flower. It is reached by a little lane (B) behind the bay and boat park, and the Coast Path that traverses it. Part of the nationally important coast heath of Holy Island, its open grassy areas, dotted with orchids, bell and ling heathers and western gorse, are maintained by grazing ponies and resident rabbits. The breeding birds are also typical, mainly meadow pipit, stonechat and linnet, with snipe using the damper grassland in winter, or usual Anglesey coast birds like chough and common raven. It's mainly a reserve for flowers like the rock-rose, heath spotted orchids, blue spring squill, yellow tormentil, dainty little heath pearlwort, pennywort, or pink ragged robin and yellow flag iris. With such flowers and aromatic mats of wild thyme come lots of insects, including butterflies, moths, grasshoppers, bees, hoverflies, lacewings, midges, beetles, ants, spiders and the like.

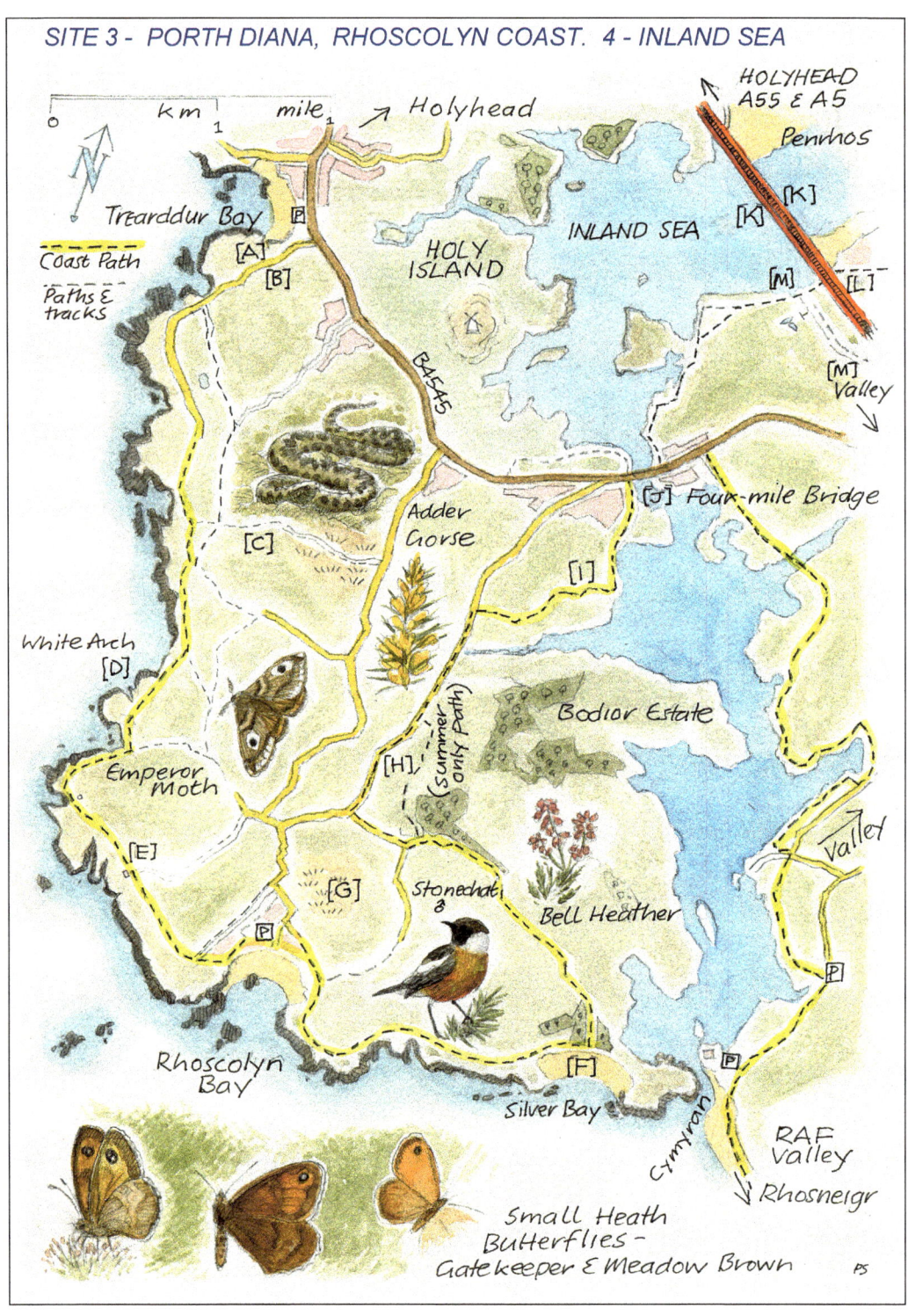

SITE 3 - PORTH DIANA, RHOSCOLYN COAST. 4 - INLAND SEA

Holyhead

HOLYHEAD
A55 & A5

Penrhos

INLAND SEA

[K] [K]

0 km 1 mile 1

N

Trearddur Bay [P]

Coast Path

Paths &
tracks

[A]

[B]

HOLY
ISLAND

[M] [L]

[M] Valley

B4545

[J] Four-mile Bridge

Adder
Gorse

[C]

[I]

White Arch
[D]

Bodior Estate

Emperor
Moth

[H] (Summer only Path)

[E]

[G]

Stonechat

Bell Heather

[P]

[P]

Rhoscolyn
Bay

[F]

Valley

[P]

Cymyran

RAF
Valley

Rhosneigr

Silver Bay

Small Heath
Butterflies -
Gatekeeper & Meadow Brown

PS

The most unusual butterfly among the commoner species, like common and small blue, is the small pearl-bordered fritillary. The seasonal 'falls' of painted ladies can also be spectacular, while resident six-spot burnet and cinnabar moths are also abundant. Yet you are more likely to see the large, bright green caterpillar of the striking emperor moth than the adult insect itself. Other insects here include the common field, green and mottled grasshoppers, or the various bumble and – hopefully – numbers of otherwise dwindling honey bee; or tiger, sexton and violet ground beetles, and several species of ladybirds. The keen will doubtless find many more insects than can be mentioned here!

Note the busy Trearddur Bay is sometimes a good place to see exotic winter visitors like long-tailed duck, scaup, goldeneye and great northern diver, among the commoner diving red-breasted mergansers, great cormorants and shags. In winter, the rocky headlands and skerries typically host purple sandpiper and pied turnstones. The usual gull species, too, although the lesser black-backed is mainly summer, and the now poorly named common gull, which is mainly winter. Such typical coast heath also has common lizards, adders and slow-worms, many of which sun themselves on rocky outcrops, especially on spring mornings as they awaken from winter torpor. Adders usually hear you long before you see them and are off. Note also their massive colour range, from very dark to light, usually according to sex.

The Coast Path continues southwards, rejoining the cliffs before eventually pitching up at the little yachty village of Rhoscolyn. It's a splendid, undulating coastline, dotted with coves and cliffs, all with typical coast F&F. An undoubted

Bwa Gwyn.

highlight is the White Arch, or Bwa Gwyn (D), made of rapidly dumped and metamorphosed Pre-Cambrian pale sandstone. There is a little marsh to bypass first (C), formerly noted for birds like reed warbler, whitethroat, reed bunting, little owl, sand and house martin, swallow and swift, although both cuckoo and yellowhammer are now sadly rarer. Next, the rather marshy St Gwenfaen's Well and the coast gets even more spectacular – and dangerous. Below the Coastguard Lookout (E), several precipitous ravines can host peregrine, chough, common raven and shag. Note also the offshore islets, one topped with a beacon warning of shallow seas and treacherous reefs.

Rhoscolyn Bay has a good beach, pub and several camp sites, before the ACP heads away from the coast before rejoining it at Traeth Gwyn, or Silver Bay (F), opposite Valley Airfield. There is a small marsh here, too (G), noted for comparative rarities like summer reed warbler and cuckoo, and occasional barn owl. The Coast Path continues northwards by largely bypassing the large and private Bodior estate – note a small section at (H) that is open in the summer – before ending up at Four-mile Bridge (J) on the valley road. Interestingly, I saw my first nightjar here – if in 1960, and rarely since on Môn – and that this final bit of the Cymyran Strait (I) Coast Path is rather boggy.

ACP, NWWT, Geo-Môn

SITE 4: INLAND SEA AND FOUR-MILE BRIDGE
OS reference SH 270-783

This large enclosed tidal lagoon is a Marine Protected Area, accessed from both north and south by the Coast Path along its western edge. The attractive little Four-mile Bridge (J) – noted for summer shoals of grey mullet as well as views – lies to the south and the Stanley Embankment (K) to the north. This is adjacent to Penrhos Country Park (Site 5), but the sea is also accessed over the busy A5 road opposite a garage (L). The embankment was built in the nineteenth century by Thomas Telford for the A5, then the London–Holyhead train line, joining Holy Island to mainland Anglesey and recently widened for the A55. This has resulted in the attractive enclosed lagoon and a splendid place for all sorts of F&F, with its wooded, rocky surrounds, strong tidal currents and both sandy and muddy shores. Unfortunately, this is also an area popular with water sports, so the Arctic terns that used to breed on the little islets have long gone. Yet, it is still a great place to watch all three regular summer species of terns, Arctic, common and sandwich, especially when fishing by the in-and-outflow (K) under the embankment.

Such shallow shores host a whole range of waders and waterfowl, or the grey herons and little egrets nesting on the far wooded shore. These include oystercatcher, redshank and greenshank, curlew, whimbrel (mainly summer only), ringed plover, dunlin, and sometimes large flocks of lapwing, golden plover, or knot – the latter three mainly in winter. Common sandpipers use the shores in spring and early autumn, with the even rarer wood sandpiper and odd wintering green sandpiper also a possibility. Ospreys are a recent and welcome recoloniser, regularly fishing on Anglesey during the summer. Their success in North Wales is self-made, although they still need protection from that bizarre anachronism – the egg-collector. That goes for the red kite, too, another charismatic recoloniser of Môn.

Peregrine falcons. *Above:* Female feeding young, South Stack. *Below:* Adults by North Stack.

Lapwing/green plover, golden plover and grey plover.

The waterfowl here are usually notable, with good numbers of shelduck, red-breasted merganser, goldeneye, great-crested and little grebe (plus regular winter black-necked & Slavonian), mute swan, Anglesey's two introduced geese (Canada and greylag), and winter flocks of wigeon and wild brent geese that alternate between here and Penrhos between tides. Note diving sea fowl are most likely at the north end of the sea, and best viewed by telescope from (M). Other winter waterfowl include the beautiful long-tailed duck, scaup and great northern diver, with spoonbill and great white egret increasingly dropping in at any season, particularly the shallower southern bays near Four-mile Bridge and the prominent windmill.

Red squirrels are also doing well here, as they are all over Anglesey since the recent reintroduction, although naturally confined to the (private) wooded north-western shores or the public woods over at Penrhos (Site 5). It is the unusual (for Anglesey) marine biology here that makes it a protected area, with all three British species of eelgrass (*Zostera*), which is so attractive to low tide, grazing wildfowl like brent geese, wigeon and pintail. This is also just the sort of partially sheltered, seagrass environment that our tiny long-snouted seahorses like to hide in (don't worry, their bizarre beauty can be seen close-up at Anglesey Sea Zoo, like the similar pipe fish). The sea is also important for its tide-swept algae (seaweed) and combination of sand, gravel and sheltered mud environments, and intertidal salt marsh, all of which attract a wide variety of marine life such as birds, crustaceans (crabs, etc.) and arthropods (shrimps/prawns), worms, shellfish and fish. The salt marsh vegetation is typical of Môn, mainly common saltmarsh grass, sea lavender, sea beet and sea rush, marsh samphire or 'Glasswort', and the uncommon golden and rock samphires. Flowers are dominated by the usual sea thrift (pinks) and sea campion, with a little area of dune heathland. Specialists will note the dwarf rush and spiral tasselweed. Even the little rocky headlands and skerries are distinctive, with attractive catastrophically folded strata and colourful lichens.

Note the Coast Path, particularly near Four-mile Bridge, can be muddy and undulating, and that paved wheelchair access is only from (K), or a private resident's road from (M) that passes the hidden gem of a screen hide on small saltmarsh pools noted for a large variety of birds, as helpfully listed there.

MPA, SSSI, AONB

SITE 5: PENRHOS COASTAL PARK
OS reference SH 275-805

This is another very popular and bird-rich tidal and woodland reserve (A) on the other side of the embankment. Formerly part of the historic Penrhos Estate, it was first established as a preserve in the 1970s by eccentric wildlife champion

SITE 5 - PENRHOS COASTAL PARK. 6 - ALAW ESTUARY

and local 'bobby' Ken Williams, with subsequent landowner Anglesey Aluminium. Williams was known for his ornamental wildfowl pools, owl sanctuary and animal hospital, as well as protecting local F&F and active campaigning and educating, resulting in the popular place it is today. It is favoured by old Toll House café-goers and dog walkers, as well as 'birders' and squirrel watchers, with its large car park, snack-bar and toilets, and many footpaths. Parking is also by Penrhos Bay (B). Like the Inland Sea, it is part of the Beddmanerch Bay and Cymyran SSSI (Site of Special Scientific Interest) and AONB (Area of Outstanding Natural Beauty). Any threats of tourist development here promise to preserve most trees for red squirrels, or any other nature at risk, as various bat species, badgers and red foxes, swathes of flowers and their butterflies, like the speckled wood, or a diverse range of birds from great spotted woodpecker to common buzzard and kingfisher, and much more, all live here.

The coast opens out here to include the muddier Penrhos shore, so beloved of increasing numbers of wintering brent geese and other birds, the large sandy banks of Traeth y Gribin and the Alaw Estuary (Site 6), opposite. They are overlooked by the Ice Age boulder clay headland and sandy bay just to the north, boasting a special circular seat and superb sea views to the Skerries and Carmel Head (Site 49). The woods ensure there are several easy and often sheltered circular walks taking in both sea and shore, whatever the weather. The recent addition of C. F. Tunnicliffe's bird art on information boards, and other features like red squirrel feeders, all help.

Its appeal for nature watchers is year-round, although it is better in winter for birdwatching, with 250 plus light-bellied brent geese (2019 tally, and note the odd, rarer dark-bellied form) often right in front of the car park with many other shorebirds. Waders are dominated at most seasons by oystercatcher, curlew, redshank and dunlin, with some whimbrel, bar- or black-tailed godwit and snipe, the odd greenshank, grey plover, spotted redshank or ruff, in both passage and winter plumages. Large winter flocks of knot, or green and golden plover, are also probable. Just as on many other Anglesey estuaries, curlew sandpiper are also an autumn

Wigeon.

speciality, as well as the odd little stint or grey phalarope. Turnstones, and sometimes purple sandpipers, also like these rocky headlands and rocks, if mainly in winter.

Shelduck are here for most of the year, if breeding numbers are currently down, with hundreds of winter wigeon, teal and red-breasted mergansers, plus goldeneye, in addition to the omnipresent mallard, odd winter pintail and resident flocks of Canada and greylag geese. Grey herons and little egrets naturally occur, with great cormorant and shag common too, as well as the divers they so often resemble. Divers like the huge great northern or the odd black- or red-throated, as well as good numbers of great crested grebes, usually with one or two of the smaller Slavonian and black-necked, or even the odd red-necked. Note the subtle differences between the grebes, and that they sometimes stay on into beautiful breeding dress.

This applies to several passage birds, especially waders like spotted redshank, knot and sanderling, resulting in the patchy plumages often observed. The fishing terns in summer are another draw, although you have to walk out onto the Cob or road footpath itself to see them close-up, by the outflow (K) with its racing jade and white currents. Currently they are dominated by common terns, but all three regular species are possible, with the very occasional roseate or little tern. As we would expect, all five regular gull species are present, although the common often just winters, currently with dozens of Mediterranean gulls, and the lesser black-backed largely summers.

Grey mullet and Atlantic bass dominate the fish species. In the quiet Alaw Estuary opposite (C), plaice are also common among the other inshore 'flatties', dab and flounder. The wide sand banks have a whole range of vital 'food' species, from lesser sand eels to various shellfish like razor clams, common cockles and pink tellin species, and worms like lugworm and small white ragworm.

The woodland and hedgerow F&F also contains a diverse number of species, including the aforementioned ones, especially the latest draw – red squirrels – and various bats, mice, shrews, the odd otter and evening polecat. The berries and nuts from sloe, hawthorn and hazel, plus brambles, are another important food source for all sorts of wildlife. Flowers from late winter onwards include prolific numbers of snowdrops, lesser celandines, primroses, bluebells, daffodils and especially wild garlic ('Ramsoms'), marsh marigold, and several fern species like royal and hart's tongue. Fungi, for whatever reason, are not particularly prolific here, aside from common saprophytic ones like sulphur tuft or various brackets.

There is a wide range of the usual woodland/garden birds, from summer warblers like willow and garden warbler, chiff-chaff and blackcap to tawny owl, ring-necked pheasant, wood pigeon, jay, magpie, nuthatch, treecreeper, all four usual tits, finches including bullfinch, the two thrushes and blackbird, robin, goldcrest, dunnock, starling and wren. House sparrows are still here, if only locally common on Anglesey, dependent on bird tables in lieu of the so-called 'weed' seeds. Greenfinches are now uncommon but seemingly recovering after their parasitic Trichomonosis disease. As with squirrel pox among reds, regular feeder cleaning is vital to help stem these problems.

Summer whitethroat and sedge warbler, with resident reed buntings, prefer damp margins and scrubbier areas, while stonechat, linnet, pied wagtail and the two pipits can all be found out on the cliffs or headland – passing whinchat too occasionally. Peregrine and kestrel, chough and common raven, are always likely on rocky coasts, with large flocks of other corvids like jackdaw, carrion crow and some rooks gathering, especially in winter.

SITE 6: ALAW ESTUARY
OS reference SH 295-805

Alaw Estuary (C) is a superb, winding little estuary with its own large coastal dune and saltmarsh area. There is limited parking nearby in Llanfachraeth or by the large Gorad housing estate. Please note, no parking, or even turning, at (D), or the inland footpath access (E). The ACP now skirts most of its meandering south-eastern shore, before crossing a new, historically decorated footbridge (F). The north-west shoreline is also accessible from here. The estuary has most of the species already mentioned for the bay as a whole, with otters regularly using the little catchment rivers to gain access to places like Llyn Alaw, or follow fish like grey mullet or silver eel upstream.

It also has a good record of attracting uncommon or elusive birds like wood sandpiper, jack snipe, corncrake, common quail, and yellow wagtail, or pioneering and no doubt future breeders such as spoonbill and great white egret. Small numbers of late summer/autumn greenshank can often be found roosting by the bridge where the Afon Alaw branches, with occasional green sandpiper along with the usual snipe, redshank, teal and kingfisher. The more open sandy shoreline and dune edge is also attractive to the likes of the odd snow bunting, shore/horned lark and Lapland bunting, but they can be very unobtrusive when scuttling among the grasses or high tide flotsam and jetsam.

Yet that's interesting in itself, with dogfish (renamed catshark) 'Mermaids Purse' egg cases, bundles of pale whelk egg cases, cuttlefish 'bones', various crab shells, jellyfish, endless shells and feathers, sea urchins, shiny brown tropical 'Sea-Beans', driftwood encrusted with strange, dangly necked goose barnacles, and, unfortunately, lots of plastic and even several invasive marine species.

Shore, edible and spider crabs.

Like virtually any coast site in western Britain, assorted avian 'mega-ticks' can also be found – if by no means typical as many are off-course or storm-bound – like 2018s superb male red-footed falcon, or recent black stork and lesser yellowlegs. And now (November 2019) there is a glossy ibis in the damp field pool beloved of ducks and waders, right by the main road.

ACP, SSSI, AONB, Cymyran SSSI

SITE 7: VALLEY WETLANDS
OS reference SH 313-76

This is one of Anglesey's two flagship RSPB wetlands, the other being Cors Ddyga (Site 13). Both naturally share similar species of birds and lots of other F&F, including bittern, marsh harrier, cettis warbler, water vole, flowering rush and northern marsh orchid. There are four main lakes and several smaller pools, small streams or marshy areas, and all are rich in wildlife. A wide network of paths traverse the area, if of varying bogginess and accessibility – note the main RSPB car park and information boards at (A), by RAF Valley Camp & Airport. The first thing that strikes the eye beyond the main water body of Llyn Penrhyn (A) is an undulating area rich in vegetation and rocky outcrops, with most of the usual waterbirds – swans, geese, ducks, grebes, rails, herons, egrets, etc. – associated with Anglesey. Much of the reserve is SSSI, including Llyn Traffwll (B) behind the RAF complex, and wetlands along the little Afon Crigyll, partly viewable from the back road by a B&B's pools, or the Tywyn Trewan Common tracks (C) (this typical gorsey heath recently (2019) hosted six wintering short-eared owls, and also overlooks parts of Cors Crigyll).

There's also an important historical aspect with a very rich Bronze and Iron Age haul of votive offerings to the gods, like swords, shields, spears, cauldrons, sickles, chariot parts and even iron slave shackles, dredged from the peat and Llyn Cerrig Bach (D) (this little pool also allows coarse fishing).

Aside from the modern instruments of war at the nearby airfield, the wetlands now host the more elegant flight of returning marsh harriers and summer ospreys, as well as the loud, explosive song of Cetti's warblers, all characteristic of several Anglesey marshes, or 'Cors'. However, another not-so-popular import was man-made, the American ruddy duck, if now extirpated here and throughout Britain. This not always popular eradication was caused by its interbreeding with the far rarer Eurasian white-headed duck in Spain. Although older guides still list Valley as a stronghold for ruddys, there are plenty of other wildfowl to see, with important numbers of breeding ducks like shoveller, gadwall, teal, pochard, tufted and the usual mallard, with mute Swan and the rowdy Canada and greylag geese. Great crested and little grebes still delight with their unique breeding displays, and, in the dabchick's case, far-carrying whinnying call. Not that it can compete with the husky and penetrating 'boom' of Anglesey's returning bitterns. The likes of the RSPB have put a lot of effort into planting reed beds for them, largely phragmites reeds, as at Cors Ddyga (Site 13) and NRW's Cors Erddreiniog (Site 29). Grey heron and little egret are also here, no doubt to be joined in the not-so-distant future by cattle and great white egrets, purple heron and spoonbill. They can all be found on Anglesey wetlands nowadays, if somewhat irregularly.

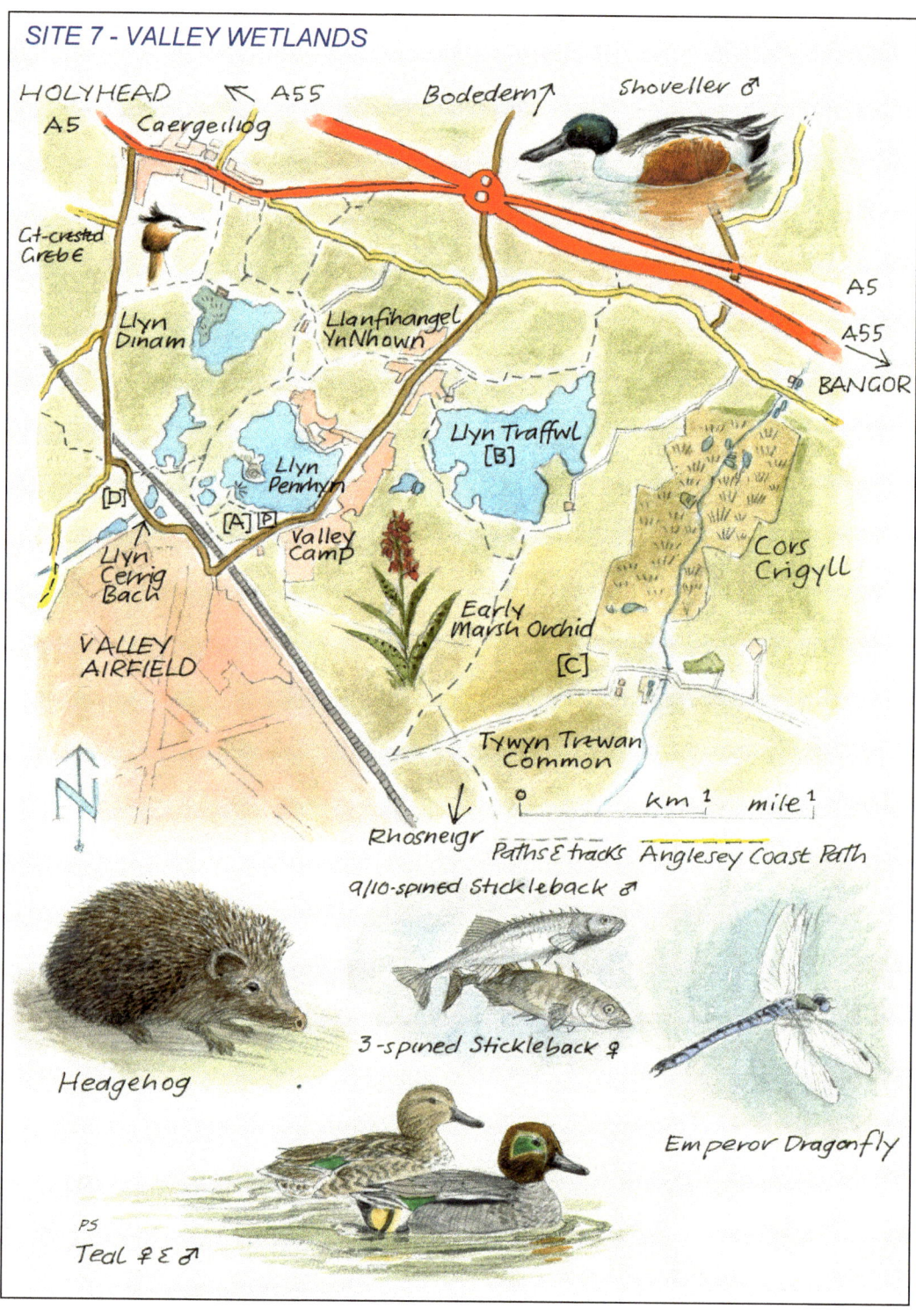

SITE 7 - VALLEY WETLANDS

HOLYHEAD   ← A55   Bodedern↗   Shoveller ♂

A5   Caergeiliog

Gt-crested Grebe

Llyn Dinam

Llanfihangel YnNhown

A5

A55

BANGOR

Llyn Traffwl [B]

Cors Crigyll

[D]

Llyn Penrhyn

[A] [B]

Llyn Cerrig Bach

Valley Camp

Early Marsh Orchid

[C]

VALLEY AIRFIELD

N

Tywyn Trewan Common

km ¹   mile ¹

Rhosneigr

Paths & tracks   Anglesey Coast Path

9/10-spined Stickleback ♂

3-spined Stickleback ♀

Hedgehog

Emperor Dragonfly

PS
Teal ♀ & ♂

As for the so-called 'moorhen' ('mere-hen' actually) and coot (far more present in winter), their nests are predated by everything from carrion crow and grey heron to red fox and otter, even gulls. I have even seen a weasel chasing their close relative, the water rail, although that's a reed bed bird we usually only hear, their harsh grunts and squeals a giveaway. Winter is the best time to see them, or over at the Spinnies near Bangor, or RSPB Conwy. The waterbirds are completed by winter visitors like goldeneye and wigeon, sub-Arctic whooper and the odd Bewick's swans, if in varying numbers, arriving from late October onwards, with various sea fowl. The gorgeous male long-tailed duck, which spent long enough here to change between equally splendid summer and winter plumages, was an exception. Like the gorgeous summer plumage, red-necked phalarope occasionally drop in, although the grey phalarope is commoner, usually in winter or juvenile dress. With the sea so close and some species also liking freshwater, common terns and others like black and white-winged black terns and whiskered can also show on Môn waters.

The birds are completed by a typical array of wetland, scrub and rough ground species; the wet margins, willows and reeds are dominated in the summer by reed, sedge and grasshopper warblers, with whitethroat and the odd elusive lesser whitethroat, or cuckoo, and good numbers of feeding swallows, swifts, sand and house martins over the waters. Resident species include lapwing and common snipe, Cetti's warbler, reed bunting, skylark, meadow pipit, stonechat, linnet, redpoll, chaffinch and goldfinch, the diminishing yellowhammer, some stock doves, raptors like peregrine, common buzzard, sparrowhawk and largely winter marsh and hen harriers, merlin and short-eared owls. Little owls, like barn owls, are regularly seen nearby at least, but littles are declining for reasons not yet clear, as elsewhere in Britain. Some starlings breed, if more likely to be seen at wetlands in large flocks in the winter, as at sites 13 and 29.

Water voles are yet another nationally endangered resident, with released and escapee mink the main problem, which is currently being addressed by many, like the Anglesey Water Vole Project. (*Wind in the Willows* didn't help, describing the goofy little vegetarian vole as 'Ratty'. The very different, pointy-faced brown rat is also here, as virtually everywhere there is water and civilisation.) Note that

Cuckoo.

any little, black and white nocturnal rodents are water shrews, with plenty of their browner common and pygmy shrew kin, plus short-tailed field and bank voles and field mice in the drier areas. Bats, like common and soprano pipistrelles, or brown long-eared bat, are fairly common wherever there is water, and hence lots of insects like caddis, stone and mayfly, mosquitoes and moths. Daubenton's bats, although uncommon here, snatch small insects off the surface. In the drier, open areas there is always a chance of brown hare, as are the usual hedgehog, red fox, rabbit, stoat, weasel, polecat, mole and, increasingly, as on most Anglesey wetlands, otters, if largely nocturnal. The lake will typically hosts lots of 'coarse' fish like rudd, roach, perch and silver eels, with common frog and toad, and newts like palmate in some of the shallower pools.

Likewise, any wetland has good numbers of large insects. The most conspicuous are the butterflies, moths, dragonflies and damselflies. Dragonfly species include hawkers like the uncommon hairy dragonfly and southern hawker, bright red (male) ruddy darter, or blue-tailed, common and variable damselflies, with banded, and the appropriately named beautiful demoiselle. Pond dipping will doubtless reveal their fearsome tadpole and fish-snapping larvae alongside a usual array of water beetles, or exotica like water scorpion, water spider and 'swan' or freshwater mussels. Butterflies are represented here by specialities like pearl-bordered fritillary among the usual gatekeeper, small heath, common and small blue butterflies, or six-spot burnet, silver Y and magpie moths. As usual, there are far more species than can be mentioned here.

Valley's riches are very much dependent on its vegetation, such as the large stands of phragmites or common reed and various rushes that surround most pools, including pretty yellow flag iris, and a whole range of plants like the beautiful flowering rush, or eight-stamened waterwort, hop sedge, marsh fern, bogbean, white and yellow lilies and pink-flowering water bistort. Willows and alder predictably grow on the edges of many pools, and typically shelter birds like warblers, tits and reed bunting. Field and meadow flowers are also a big feature, particularly lots of (often hybridising) northern and early marsh-orchids in the meadows, along with yellow rattle, ragged robin, mayflower (cuckooflower), meadowsweet, purple loosestrife, etc.. The rocky outcrops, which make such good viewpoints for the lakes, have their own attraction, from bright summer heathers and gorses to colourful lichens – and a convenient bench on the main one.

Walking further afield brings you back to the Coast Path at several points: either the beautiful Cymyran Strait and hence north to Four-mile Bridge or south along Rhosneigr's busy surfing beach. Amazingly, terns still manage to nest on the little RSPB-managed Ynys Feirig isles (Site 8), and the likes of Lapland bunting can show up anywhere on our autumn shores, with the odd American golden plover sometimes nearby among the whirling flocks of green and golden plover.

RSPB, SSSI, ACP

Site 8: Llyn Maelog and Rhosneigr
OS reference SH 325-730

This largish lake (A) is half fringed by thick stands of reeds – hence its attraction to wintering bittern and marsh harrier – where you can see many of the usual

SITE 8 - LLYN MAELOG & RHOSNEIGR

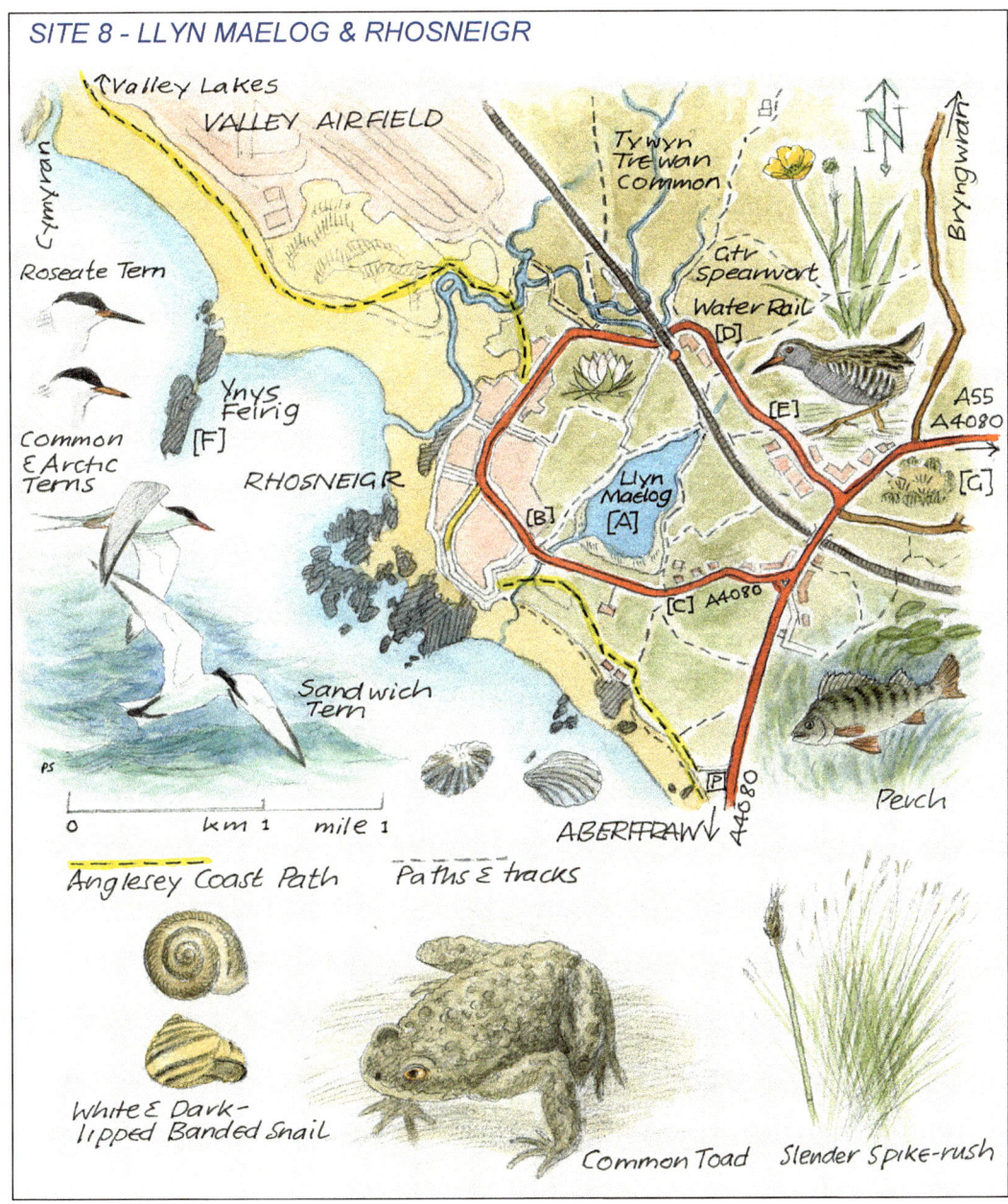

Valley Lakes
VALLEY AIRFIELD
Cymyran
Roseate Tern
Common & Arctic Terns
Ynys Feirig [F]
RHOSNEIGR
Sandwich Tern
PS
0   km 1   mile 1

Tywyn Tre wan Common
Ctr Spearwort
Water Rail [D]
[E]
Llyn Maelog [A]
[B]
[C] A4080
A55 A4080
[G]
Perch
P A4080
ABERFFRAW

Bryngwran

Anglesey Coast Path   Paths & tracks

White & Dark-lipped Banded Snail   Common Toad   Slender Spike-rush

Anglesey waterbirds mostly year-round. Fortunately it can be overlooked from two public footpaths, accessed from (B) (C) and (D) (E), around most of the shore, even if they are rather boggy and rocky in places. Both roads have parking, if limited. The lake was formerly important for its islet of breeding black-headed gulls, as well as Mediterranean gull, before being overrun by water-sports – as on the Inland Sea. This is also a fishing lake, if limited mainly to the south-western shore by the A4080. Nevertheless, the 'Meds', the adult showing smart all-white wings, truly black heads and heavier red bills, are increasing on Anglesey, as at Cemlyn (Site 46). The waterbirds predictably reflect a healthy fish, insect and plant life, and include grey heron, little egret, great cormorant, mute swan, Canada and greylag geese, shelduck, shoveller, gadwall, pochard, tufted duck, mallard, red-breasted merganser, coot, water rail, great-crested and little grebes, which are joined in winter by goldeneye and (increasingly on Anglesey waterways) goosanders, with the odd scaup or even smew. Bittern and marsh harrier mainly winter, with five or so bitterns here over the odd hard winter, even fishing the little streams. Water rails also show here, while the more mobile harriers come and go at will, joined in loose concord with winter hen harrier. Short-eared owls are also a winter possibility, with barn and little owls breeding nearby, the close proximity of sand dunes and typically small, boggy and 'unimproved' pastures and all their small mammals tempting such aerial predators. There are also red fox, stoat, weasel and probably polecat too.

Naturally, the reedy and scrubby margins attract the usual summer coterie of warblers, with the rattly and repetitive 'songs' of sedge and reed and the Whitethroat's nasal churring and scratchy refrain being a good giveaway. Attractive reed buntings are resident, swapping melody for looks with their pathetic little, 'cheep-cheep-chink' song. Stonechats, too, can usually be heard 'chacking' anywhere there is rough and rocky ground, heather or gorse, like the area at the north end of the lake. Grey partridge used to be common, but nowadays you are more likely to see the deliberately imported red-legged or 'French' partridge, commonly bred for shooting, as with the many (ring-necked) pheasants on the island.

Cuckoos should also be present in summer, what with their favourite host, reed warbler, being found here, but nowadays this is by no means reliable. The starling roost is reliable, at least in recent winters, if mainly after New Year when they initially gather by the little village of Llanfaelog for their mesmerising aerobatics, even featuring on *Autumnwatch* in 2016 via local wildlife cameraman Jesse Wilkinson. As for the raptors that often accompany any such gathering, peregrines can always be relied on, plus common buzzard, sparrowhawk and winter merlin attempting to pick off the odd straggler. Kestrels and regular summer osprey and the odd hobby make up the raptor list, although red kites are increasingly seen on Môn, and probably (2019) already breeding.

As for mammals, the most charismatic here, apart from brown hare, will be otter, and by no means as nocturnal as polecats. The huge males, or females with well-grown young, can be seen at any time of day and in virtually any water body, large or small, fresh or marine. Bats, too, are regular over the water in the evening, with at least six of Britain's regular sixteen found on Anglesey, including brown long-eared, the two pipistrelles, noctule and the odd whiskered or Daubenton's, although the latter two are still rather uncommon.

As in any wetland, the vegetation is very important when it comes to the whole interdependent web of F&F (or 'biotope'). The large reed beds are mainly common/phragmites reed, although there are small numbers of flowering rush, slender spike rush and shoreweed, alongside other water plants like white water lilies, Autumnal water starwort and spiked water milfoil. There is also seven species of pondweed here, like the horned, perfoliate or lesser, but they vary hugely. Some are broad-leaved and floating, thereby superficially resembling another common and pretty water plant on Anglesey: the pink flowering water or amphibious bistort. Flowering water forget-me-not and water mint are also common, unlike the striking, yellow-flowered greater spearwort and lesser water plantain. Note that all water plants are not so benign, or even edible, like the mint, as 'Eutrophication' or nutrient over-enrichment of such lakes by agricultural or human by-products can produce the deadly phyto-plankton of 'Blue-Green Algae' that is so dangerous to bathing or drinking dogs (although some 204 species of algae are recorded here!). Adders are also fairly common, although again I must stress they are quite shy and rarely seen, apart from when found sunbathing.

The fish here are both natural, like the migratory silver sewin or sea trout and its mysterious, non-seagoing kin, the brown trout, alongside bream, roach, rudd, perch and predatory pike, some especially introduced for fishing. Silver eels (although yellow/green in freshwater) are doubtless present – otter, grey heron, red-breasted merganser, goosander and great cormorant regularly catch them all over Anglesey. As for the two commonest stickleback forms, the freshwater red-breasted or three-spined, and the black-breasted, nine/ten-spined of more brackish waters, they might both be here. Other water life is equally rich, from daphnia to water beetles of all sizes, to damselfly and dragonfly larvae, water snails to leeches – if not the larger, rare medicinal leech as found over at Site 28. Anglesey does have some water spiders with their amazing underwater air-bubble homes, but huge numbers of land spiders, like the garden or common orb-weaver family, whose dewy or frosty webs so often artfully drape gorse or grasses. As for snails, the striking ramshorn snail and commoner great (and small) pond snails are all possible on Anglesey, with at least the large 'Swan' or freshwater mussel found here. Don't forget land snails, either, as the pretty, variably coloured – red, yellow or brown, or all three – banded (dark or white-lipped) snail is locally common, as is the large brown 'Roman snail'. I should also mention all the slugs, mainly orange or large black, but also the rarer and striking leopard slug – and hedgehogs like them.

Ramshorn and pond snail.

With some fifteen species of dragonflies and damselflies on Anglesey, the commoner ones at least occur here, like various hawkers or the omnipresent common blue damselfly. Butterflies include common species like small tortoiseshell, red admiral and common blue, with several grasshoppers and beetles, such as the variously patterned and coloured shield bugs, ladybirds, or showy moths like the magpie, cinnabar or brimstone in the surrounding scrub. Sadly, the cinnabar moth's current rise in numbers seems to be due to its obsession with invasive Oxford ragwort. The plants are usually covered in the red and black moth's distinctive little yellow and black-banded caterpillars, so at least there is some control of the plant going on. However, will the moths naturally control the plant, as they have been deliberately introduced onto other continents to do?

Talking of problems, the little offshore RSPB Ynys Feirig reserve islets (F), just down the road from Maelog, is where Arctic and common terns still breed despite the very heavy water traffic all around them. Sandwich terns are also found fishing up and down this coast in summer, while a variety of waders use the busy beaches, especially after storms. The rocky headland and islets to the west of the town are especially attractive to waders and the usual gulls. Oystercatchers are typical and resident, whereas the charming little 'scuttles' of sanderling, dunlin, weed and stone-flipping turnstones are largely winter. Note the neat little wetland opposite Bryncoed Garage (G), good for summer warblers. Summer also can see sand martins nesting in the dunes, depending on the availability of natural eroding sand cliffs. They can also nest in the boulder clay cliffs by Porth Nobla, to the south by Porth Trecastell, or Cable Bay. Note that the Coast Path south officially follows the main A4080 road from there on, turning off for the Anglesey Motor Racing Circuit, before branching off that for Port Cwyfan – and that the church on the heavily eroded little islet was originally some 100 yards inland when it was first built in the twelfth century!

ACP, SSSI, RSPB

SITE 9: ABERFFRAW BAY AND COMMON, LLYN CORON
OS reference SH 355-688

This interesting area is dominated by rolling sand dunes that host a wealth of typical flora and fauna, if sometimes subtle, from flowers, shrubs, fungi, mosses and lichens, insects, birds, mammals, reptiles, and amphibians to a rich fringe of marine biology. This is typical if largely hidden behind the lofty sand hills, by means of an open 'storm beach', rugged headland of Trwyn y Wylan (B) and winding little sandy estuary down to the historic 'Princes of Gwynedd' village of Aberffraw (A). The dunes are also adjacent to the rich wildfowl and 'game' fishing lake of Llyn Coron (C). The Coast Path from Porth Cwyfan first traverses the headland, noted for grey seals that sometimes pup nearby, before reaching the village and crossing the iconic stone bridge. Picturesque it might be, but it only dates to the eighteenth century, whereas Aberffraw is claimed as the historic seat and proud capital of the entire Kingdom of Gwynedd in the early Middle Ages, under such famed leaders as Llewellyn the Great. Now a whole web of footpaths lead out from the bridge, if much of the dune system is open access. Note the footpaths on either side of Llyn Coron are often boggy or overgrown, and include a diversion by a charming little ford to the east (D).

SITE 9 - ABERFFRAW BAY & COMMON, LLYN CORON

Soar ↑

A55
A5 ↑ Bethel

Brown
Hare

Short-eared
Owl

[E]

Llyn
Coron
[C]

[D]

MALLTRAETH

Afon Ffraw

Llangadwaladwr

RHOSNEIGR
← A4080

P

P

Common Blue &
Sea
Holly

Skylark ♂
& Whinchat

ABERFFRAW

P

F

Bodorgan
Estate

[AC]

[B]

Aberffraw
Bay

Short-tailed
Vole

Porth
Cwyfan

Anglesey
Coast Path

N

PS

1 mile   1 km   0

Paths & tracks

Slowworm

Sea Spurge

Wintergreen

The birds are predictably varied, from sea to freshwater, dune and field. Common raven regularly roll and tumble in the updrafts over the tallest dunes as common buzzard and kestrel hang on the winds, seeking small mammals like short-tailed field voles or field mice. These appear so plentiful that I recently saw a diurnal (day-hunting) barn owl catch three voles in no more than twenty-five minutes! And at the moment (December 2019), over twelve short-eared owls are wintering, their numbers also linked to high, cyclical vole numbers in their sub-Arctic breeding grounds. Other wind players here include chough, carrion crow, jackdaw, rook and magpie, all seeking out insects, small mammals or reptiles in the shorter grass areas. The plentiful gorse and tall, dried umbellifers often have bright stonechats chacking from them – plus occasional spring whinchat – when breeding linnets share the scrub. Another noticeable bird in spring is the bright and upright wheatear, strutting about the shorter grasses especially by the back road to Llyn Coron. Note a few do breed on the island, and some passing by will be of the brighter, Greenland 'race'. Other spring passerines include cuckoo, whitethroat, sedge and willow warbler, chiff-chaff and blackcap, as well as lots of hirundines (swallow, house and sand martin) and swifts over the lake. Sadly, former residents like yellowhammer and tree sparrow are now uncommon. Skylarks, meadow pipits and pied wagtails are still predictable and year-round, as virtually everywhere else on Anglesey, and joined by coastal rock pipits or the odd water pipit and small flocks of white wagtails in spring. Sand martins sometimes nest in the summer dunes and hunt insects over Llyn Coron, often one of the first places to see hirundines in the spring. Reed buntings like the willowy fringes of the lake and outlet stream, plus the usual garden/woodland fringe birds, while red-legged and now returning grey partridges use the surrounding fields.

Locally we even have common flocks of house sparrows, no doubt due to lots of 'weed' seeds, and the few greenfinch survivors of their specific disease. Winter can also see the stream's willowy fringes alive with flocks of starlings, fieldfares and redwings, and tiny goldcrest, typically foraging with restless flocks of long-tailed and other tits (plus chaffinch, goldfinch and the odd pair of bullfinch). More sporadic and unpredictable, wintering merlin and hen harrier sometimes join the other raptors, like sparrowhawk, peregrine, and now marsh harrier – all good signs of an area with a rich 'natural larder'.

Llyn Coron has many of the usual waterfowl, with diving ducks (tufted duck and pochard) and dabblers (mallard, gadwall and shoveller) predominating, and largely from autumn onwards teal, wigeon, shelduck, goldeneye, red-breasted merganser, with goosander in flocks of up to 40 plus – another new phenomena on Môn. The odd smew, smart black and white male, or 'redhead' (female or immature), winters, if not as regularly now. As usual, the noisiest and most predominant waterbirds are the big flocks of Canada and greylag geese (some white-fronted geese are always possible in winter, plus the odd barnacle, pink-footed or snow goose) in the surrounding fields, as well as winter wader flocks. These are mostly lapwing, golden plover, curlew and oystercatcher, as well as varying numbers of common snipe and the odd jack snipe in damper, juncus-y hollows. Bittern now winter regularly in the reeds, some from England or even the Continent, although they now breed nearby (Site 13). Other birds regularly seen

♀&♂ Red-breasted Merganser
♂ & ♀ Goosander

Red-breasted merganser and goosander.

are mute swan (whooper are possible in winter), great cormorant, great crested grebe – more in winter, like coot – and 'mere-hen', little grebe and lots of loafing gulls. The lake's rushy edges and boggy margins regularly host grey heron, little egret, water rail, kingfisher, grey wagtail and winter woodcock. Green sandpiper also winter or drop in, with possibly common sandpiper, as in the spring. Note also the little marsh at (E), its eastern edges partially viewable from footpaths, which sometimes host wintering hen harrier, as well as barn owl and the usual wetland F&F.

Many of the aforementioned waders are driven inland by high tides or gales, or may only feed on the shore at low tide, as some gulls, waders and corvids do. Others rarely venture far, like turnstone, redshank, dunlin, sanderling or purple sandpiper that winter on the rocks, estuary or beach, or the various terns, gulls, auks, gannets or Manx shearwater that fish or pass just offshore for much of the year. Other passing sea fowl, such as common scoter, skuas, petrels, divers and grebes, mainly choose to winter around our coasts, but virtually any of them can end up on freshwater after severe gales.

As for mammals, brown hare and rabbit are the most likely to be seen, along with red fox, stoat, weasel, mole, polecat and otter, all of varying degrees of invisibility, or simply more nocturnal. A polecat's striking gold mask in the headlights is a giveaway as they dice with death on the fast dunes road. Like stoats and weasels, though, they can occasionally put on a highly visible daytime dance, although whether to hypnotise prey, display or simply joie-de-vivre is unclear. Happily, brown hares, also famed for their 'Mad-March' performances, are common here, despite illegal hunting. As for smaller mammals, as already noted bank or short-tailed voles are common, with the usual range of others from field mice to pygmy shrews. Bats, too, are usually visible, especially by the lake, particularly pipistrelles and brown long-eared and possible Daubenton's.

The dunes are particularly well studied for their plants, which has resulted in SSSI and SAC (Special Area of Conservation) status, along with nearby Newborough (Site 12), both lying within the local AONB. A typically rich and varied UK dune system, it combines windblown, mobile sand in the fore dunes, shielding the many damp dune 'slacks' or hollows among the marram-draped hills, backed by varying degrees of grass, scrub and tree growth. There are well over 100 species of plant life here, plus fungi, mosses and lichens. The most obvious are the orchids, mainly marsh and spotted varieties, although, like many other life forms, 'interbreeding' is rife. Northern marsh orchid and early marsh orchid are both liable to cross here, as do common spotted orchid types. One of the most beautiful and easiest to ID, the bee orchid is sometimes in the drier spots here, although limestone (Sites 22 and 29) is more reliable. Pyramidal orchids are most widespread of all, apart from their usual clifftop heath habitat. As for other common flowers, the violets or pansies are particularly lovely and common, whether dune pansy or common dog or heath violet individuals, or crosses. Not for nothing is the dune pansy called 'tricolor' in Latin, for it can be yellow, white or violet, or any combination thereof.

One of the most prominent plants is the yellow-green, cactus-like spike of sea spurge or 'Euphorbia' species, commonly found in open sand among marram grass, like the equally distinct, ice-green sea holly. In the slacks we find many smaller plants including clovers, wild thyme, silverweed, round-leaved wintergreen, 'creeping' or dwarf willow sps, pink bog pimpernel, cat's ear and grasses like red fescue and dune soft brome. The dried out, egg-yellow tops of carline thistle are also distinctive. Variegated horsetail is typical of the damper areas, as in many Anglesey ditches and soggy bottoms, along with false cress, water mint and dock sps. Note the typical long green tresses of water crowfoot, which are only found in clean waters like the little Afon Ffraw, which, with the lake, also hosts brown trout and their migratory sea trout kin. As for the dreaded Oxford ragwort, Aberffraw is often awash with them, so at least expect lots of cinnabar moths.

Fungi also appear a law unto themselves, although their global underworld of tiny filaments or hyphae – the real 'world-wide-web' – is vital and interdependent with most vegetation. Apart from hundreds of slender parasol mushrooms, field or horse mushrooms, common puffballs, bright red, yellow and black dune waxcaps and fairy ring champignons, some superficially resemble crosses betwixt field, wood and Parasol, or even mini-versions of the much-prized and scaly prince mushroom. However, care is always needed, for we also have a few poisonous yellow-staining mushrooms, which strongly resemble yellowing horse or field sps, but mainly identified by a rank, sharp odour. Dunes also host many lichens and bryophytes (mosses and liverworts), especially a smaller Cladonia 'reindeer moss' species, or one of our most successful and widespread 'homalothecium' mosses, and the rare, if rather unspectacular, little green liverwort known as petalwort.

Along with all that plant life, insects are also common. Tunnelling sand wasps and mining bees are some of the most observable in the open sand, along with uncommon forms of orange and black sexton beetles, or green tiger beetles. In a good year, butterflies should include common and small blue butterflies, orange tip, meadow brown, painted ladies and small pearl-bordered fritillary. And with the damper areas, river and lake, dragonflies and damselflies, and many flies like caddis and the sedges (which trout so love!), are reasonably common, like the towering clouds of mating winter gnats. Note that there are many other species of F&F to be observed here on Anglesey, so please refer to specialist literature and organisations like the NRW and North Wales Wildlife Trust.

Orange tip butterfly.

With so any wet areas, the usual amphibians and reptiles will be found here. Adder, slow-worm, common lizard, common frog and toad, and palmate newt make up the bulk of them, but do look out for grass snake, which is uncommon on the island, but spends a lot of time in water. Great crested newts and sand lizards might also be seen, following the latter's reintroduction to various part of North Wales, as at nearby Newborough (Site 11), where the newts are fairly common. Note that the Coast Path leaves the dunes at (F), yet in bypassing the private Bodorgan Estate headland on a quiet C road, it passes through one of the best areas for brown hare and barn owl, then a very pheasant-y and tawny owl-ed wood, before rejoining the coast at Malltraeth Sands.

SSSI, SAC, AONB

SITE 10: MALLTRAETH COB POOL, CEFNI ESTUARY
OS reference SH 408-685

One of the most famous birdwatching sites on Anglesey, it's a superb area that is rightly famed for natural history and varied scenery, comprising the large estuary, saltmarsh and dunes of the Afon Cefni with the convenient shelter belt of Newborough Forest (B), and grand backdrop of Eryri-Snowdonia and Llŷn. It is often defined by the Cob, or embankment (A), that dammed the estuary of the Cefni in 1812, thus producing rich farming areas and new wildlife habitats – if also losing much. The pool created behind the Cob is still one of the best wildfowl sites on Anglesey, if mainly in winter. We can only imagine the huge estuary that was here, almost splitting Anglesey in two, although to past inhabitants it was either dangerous marsh or 'bad sands' – one explanation of the name 'Mall-Traeth' – only to be carefully waded or ferried across. As if in memory, some seabirds still use this shortcut across Anglesey. The reclamation was for both farming, peat digging and coal mining, as explained at Site 13, eventually resulting in lands rich for both us and wildlife. The fact that the twentieth century's finest all-round country artist, C. F. Tunnicliffe RA OBE, spent almost half his life here at

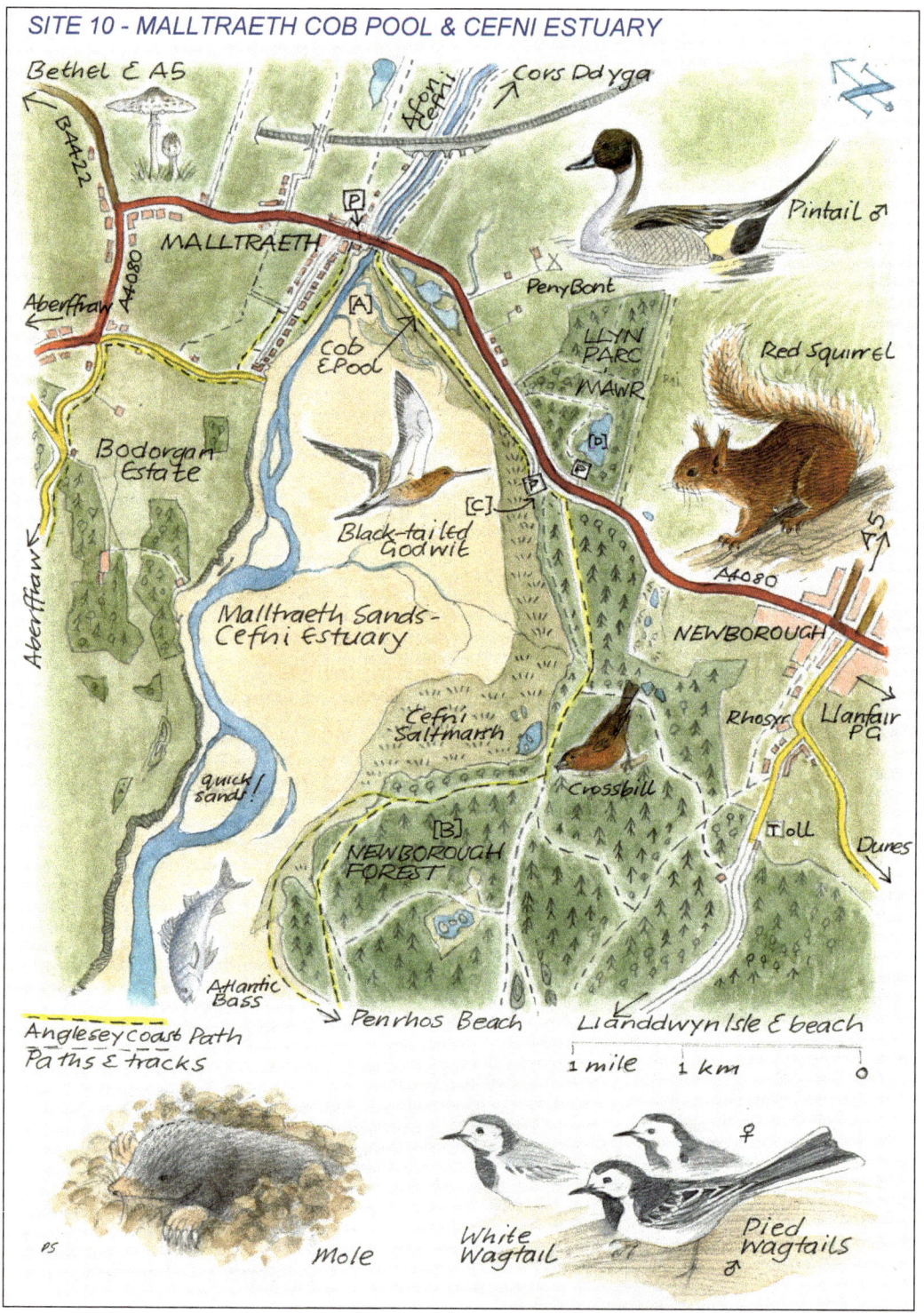

SITE 10 - MALLTRAETH COB POOL & CEFNI ESTUARY

Bethel & A5

Cors Ddyga

Afon Cefni

B4422

MALLTRAETH

Aberffraw

A4080

PenyBont

Pintail ♂

Cob E Pool

[A]

LLYN PARC MAWR

Red Squirrel

Bodorgan Estate

[D]

[C]

A5

Aberffraw

Black-tailed Godwit

A4080

Malltraeth Sands-Cefni Estuary

NEWBOROUGH

quick sand!

Cefni Saltmarsh

Crossbill

Rhosyr

Llanfair PG

[B]
NEWBOROUGH FOREST

Toll

Dunes

Atlantic Bass

Penrhos Beach

Llanddwyn Isle & beach

Anglesey coast Path
Paths & tracks

1 mile   1 km   0

PS

Mole

White Wagtail

♀

Pied Wagtails

Malltraeth, celebrating it in 'Shorelands Summer' and 'Winter' diaries, and many sketchbooks, certainly defines its allure to birdwatchers and artists. (This author/ artist recently produced a modest update on Tunnicliffe's books and the area, *Tall Tales from and Estuary*. Tunnicliffe's work can be seen at Oriel Môn and is rightly perpetuated by the Tunnicliffe Society.)

The Cob Pool is one of the first stops for most birders, and can host a rich selection of birds, winter or summer, as well as otter, grey mullet and a whole array of summer flowers including several orchids. The Coast Path runs along it, with parking at either end, but take care as it is also now a fast cycle track. Please note that on some days there might be little life on the pool, depending on tide or season. The winter ducks and waders could well be out feeding on the wide estuary when the tide is low, or feeding on fields or at its green edges on the other side of the Cob as the waters rise. One of our most elegant birds is the famous wintering pintail (averaging around 250 nowadays), along with wigeon, teal, mallard and shelduck, as well as lots of waders like curlew, oystercatcher, black-tailed godwit, redshank, common snipe, lapwing, golden plover, dunlin, ringed plover, knot and a few greenshank or spotted redshank. They are sometimes joined by the odd jack snipe, grey plover or bar-tailed godwit, which can also feed either out on the wide sands or in saltmarsh gullies, before heading for the marshes or nearby damp fields to roost. The winter wader flocks can be huge, with up to 7,000 lapwing and golden plover in colder weather, although sadly few of them breed here in North Wales, or even Britain. Whirling flocks set against the white massif of Eryri defines one of Malltraeth's most glorious winter sights, especially when sunny and frosty and all is reflected in a high morning tide.

Yet how rapidly things change, like black-tailed godwits, which only passed through in summer until recently, then 100 plus suddenly wintered, only to drop down to around a dozen since. By spring they also assume the glorious breeding plumage of several waders: burnt orange, buff, black and white. The odd ruff, bar-tailed godwit, curlew sandpiper, turnstone or sanderling can also drop by in such spring finery, or when returning south. Late summer is also the best time for the odd little stint, grey phalarope, wood sandpiper, or, more uncommon, pectoral sandpiper. We have even seen American spotted sandpiper and Eurasian white pelican here, although the red-whiskered bulbul, hooded merganser, whistling tree duck, red-tailed hawk, Eleanora's falcon and bald eagle were mainly escapees!

Other winter birds – although that term is confusing, as post-breeding lapwings begin to return in early June and others like short-eared owls don't leave until April – include kingfisher, merlin and hen harrier. Raven numbers are now far less than their record-breaking 1700 plus roost in Newborough Forest (Site 12), the large corvids mercilessly hammering such raptors year-round, whether the two harriers (including marsh), or osprey and red kite. Winter merlin, or the resident peregrine, common buzzard, kestrel, sparrowhawk and goshawk don't appear as bothered, but prospecting summer ospreys are possibly being dissuaded from breeding, just as the Welsh population otherwise grows. The shallow estuary here is ideal for the master fishers, full of flatfish like dab and flounder and summer grey mullet, as well as sea trout and Atlantic bass, and appropriate nesting trees. As for shelducks, they're resident apart from when adults leave to moult in late summer, with up to 600 returning some years in late autumn, but breeding

Kingfisher.

numbers in north-west Wales have fallen drastically. *Birds of Anglesey* recorded some 473 ducklings on Anglesey in 1992, but recently juvenile numbers on this estuary alone have gradually gone down to just one individual (2018). Yet one of their main foods, the tiny hydrobia snail, still appears plentiful. The increase in red foxes is one cause of decline, as I myself saw (through a telescope, helpless a mile away), a family of Shelducklings taken, one by one, from the edge of the saltmarsh. Mind you, everything from otter to bittern to great black-back will take the pretty little shelducklings, or any appropriately sized living thing, to feed their own young. Shelducks can be equally vicious to rival's young. Then, even the pretty little kingfishers, which come down the Cefni to winter here, are often as obstreperous, fighting viciously over prime territory by the road bridge.

'Bumpy' the curlew also currently spends much of her winter here defending the same area, as do redshank, oystercatcher, little egret and grey heron. 'Bumpy' – named for the golf ball-sized lump of back feathers at the base of her neck – is exceptional in her devotion to this 125 yards of choice mud. It obviously has all the marine worms and crabs, etc., her kind love, as she has been coming here for at least six August to spring sojourns, and once survived three peregrine stoops by crouching low at the water's edge (note, not three peregrine 'strikes', as mistakenly recorded in Mary Colwell's *Curlew Moon* book). Other regular residents here are great cormorants, as well as the odd shag and winter grey seal (even an uncommon common seal recently), which, like grey herons, love to wrestle with common eels or flatties. The livelier little egrets simply spear any little living thing within reach, from shrimps to fish to crabs. Dozens of bright wigeon are one of the most attractive winterers, feeding on the green filamentous algae of 'blanket-weed', *Enteramorpha*, or various seagrasses ('blanket-weed' is not so welcome in large, deoxygenating swathes, as at Lavan Sands, by Bangor, where it is usually a sign of 'Eutrophication' caused by agri-chemical run-off).

Dabchicks or little grebes also winter here, usually around six in number but up to twenty-four in the last hard winter (2010), with the odd immature great crested grebe. Most birds are harassed by gulls, whether herring, black-headed, great black-backed, common, or, in summer, lesser black-backed. All but the now inaccurately named common gull breed somewhere nearby. Increasingly, one or two Mediterranean or little gulls also drop in, or the two winter Arctic gulls, even the odd American ring-billed gull. Red-breasted merganser, goosander and goldeneye also regularly fish here, the latter in winter only and in declining numbers, sometimes with a smart male smew. Other winter estuarine visitors include storm-blown razorbills and guillemots, the odd massive great northern or red-throated diver, and one particular New Year's Day surprise – a great skua, using the overland marsh route to get back to the Celtic Sea. Rock and meadow pipit, pied and grey wagtails and the occasional black redstart use the bridge area, which is also a favourite hangout for our modest flock of house sparrows and a few resident starlings. Bittern can also drop into the Cob Pool, where the noisy water rail is the other lurker. Green and common sandpipers have also wintered nearby, though commoner on passage, when, in August, up to twenty-four returning commons roost here or on the 'Big-Bend' up river beyond the railway viaduct, along with around nine greenshanks, and the odd little-ringed plover. The latter have nested at Conwy RSPB.

Summer can see many of the same birds variously fishing or resting here, plus one of our first visitors of the year from March onwards: sandwich terns. Other seabirds like black guillemot, razorbill, kittiwake, and choughs are usually out by the private Gullery cliffs at the mouth of the estuary, by Penrhos Beach and dunes. Garganey is another fairly regular visitor to estuary or Cob Pool, although rarely stopping more than a few hours – just as avocets have recently done, and other pioneers like great white and cattle egret, spoonbill and ruff.

The Cob embankment itself currently hosts breeding stonechat, reed bunting, skylark, meadow pipit, linnet, sedge, grasshopper and willow warblers, whitethroat, chiff-chaff, and the usual garden/woodland birds, including blackbird, song thrush, robin, wren and dunnock, with most of the tits and finches including regular long-tailed and bullfinch. Plus great spotted woodpecker, wood pigeon, collared dove, mistle thrush, siskin and redpoll, which regularly fly over from the forest or nearby gardens, or snack on their feeders. Busy rooks and jackdaws also nest and roost here, or join the raven mega roost opposite. As for owls, barn owls are still fairly regular on the surrounding farmland. Short-eared are sporadic in winter, long-eared even more so, and little owls appear to be shadowing their mysterious national decline. That goes for cuckoos too, which, along with green woodpeckers, used to reliably provide a background soundtrack for our brief summers. Our heronry is now mainly a (little) egretry, far outnumbering their grey cousins, although that can only be clearly seen from out on the low-tide estuary near the forest. Note that the estuary has dangerous areas of quicksand. The sands also abound in common cockles, carpet shell and tellin species, along with lug and other sand worms and common mussels, various periwinkles and limpets on the rocks, and lots of sand gobies and common shrimps in the shallows. Another common shore creature is the little shrimp-like sandhopper, which are especially fond of tideline debris and the favoured prey of bird foragers.

As already mentioned, red foxes head up the commoner mammals here, although stoat and weasel are regularly seen on the Cob – and the stoats, like their mountain

Stoats – one in ermine.

kin, produce white winter ermine coats – but only when snowy. As with much of the UK's overt cleansing of rivers and cessation of hunting, otters have quickly returned and regularly leave their fishy or crabby spraints on the banks, or are seen fishing in small family groups. Eel, grey mullet, crab, flattie, amphibian, bird, mammal, swan mussel, you name it, they eat it. Brown rats are not so welcome as they also invade our homes, but we also have smaller mammals like mole, hedgehog, bank and short-tailed vole, wood and field mouse, common and pygmy shrew, and pipistrelle and other bats coming out of the nearby forest – now a great place for red squirrels (Site 12).

Common lizards are also still common, if sometimes elusive and quite varicoloured in warm browns, greens or greys – unlike the brighter yellow-green and rare sand lizard, as I once saw eaten by a kestrel here. Adders are likewise common and a favourite prey of the increasing common buzzard. Common frogs and toads, palmate, common and great crested newts all breed hereabouts, at least at adjacent Newborough. That also goes for various dragonflies, like the Red Darter, and the Cob can be good for the usual butterflies as well as common and small blue, and moths like six-spot burnet, elephant hawk moth or the emperor – although we rarely see the spectacular adults of the latter two, just their bizarrely eyed or, conversely, large green caterpillars. Other insects include the huge cockchafer or 'June bug', bloody-nose, violet ground and tiger beetles, devil's coach-horse, and lots of woodlice or pill bugs, while the Cob path often hosts good numbers of variously coloured banded snails.

Naturally, the plant life helps define everything from birds to insects, and the usual rich mix associated with Welsh estuaries, as described for the Inland Sea. Spartina is the main mud and sand flat pioneer here, with common saltmarsh grasses and sea aster, edible plants like common orache, sea purslane, sea beet, and marsh and rock samphire still all spreading. The Cob itself has a beautiful array of summer grasses from Yorkshire fog to red fescue and wild oats, different sedges and bents, plus clover and dock species, plantain, gorses, wild chives and any mats of lamb's lettuce and wild thyme that survive Coast Path herbicides. Tall vegetation requires tall mushrooms, so parasols are common including the odd field or horse mushroom. Occasionally, the lovely pink trumpets of sea bindweed snake across short grass, and where there is some shelter, tree mallow predominates. The trees are naturally stunted, and mainly elder, hawthorn and willow, which are beset with blackberry but beloved of all sorts of F&F for food and shelter. Carrion crows also nest, resulting in regular predation of pool-nesting wildfowl – although it has to be said that many other critters, like otters, also do that.

Note the little reserve of Llyn Parc Mawr Community Woodland at (D), especially famed for red squirrels and its wildfowl-rich pool.

SAC, SSSI, NRW, AONB, ACP

SITE 11: NEWBOROUGH DUNES

SITE 12: FOREST AND LLANDDWYN ISLE
OS reference SH 405-635

Newborough Dunes is another beautiful and rightly famed area, especially since the successful reintroduction of red squirrels to Newborough Forest (B), and being near to the rolling Warren dunes (C), historic Llanddwyn Island (A), several superb beaches and the sinuous Cefni and Braint Estuaries. Newborough Warren is still one of the largest and most important sand dune systems in Britain, despite half of it being afforested, and Llanddwyn Island and beaches, an extremely popular tourist area. Yet little of this existed until the huge sand dunes were formed, largely in the well documented great storm of 1331 that buried many parts of the 'new' village of Newborough in sand. In fact, much of Britain's west coast has evidence of earlier and even more catastrophic coast erosions and sand movements, especially the mid-sixth century AD event that flooded large areas of north-west Wales and rerouted the Afon Conwy. Then there's all the tree stumps that are found just offshore, as in Trearddur Bay, or from Cumbria down to Cornwall.

The Newborough area was originally named Rhosyr and another important site of the Princes of Gwynedd, and now an archaeological site linked to the Pritchard-Jones Institute in the village. Yet 'New-borough' only came about after the forcible repopulation of the people of Llanfaes by the Anglo-French Edward I, replacing their settlement with 'Beaumaris' and its bijou little castle (Site 18). Until the sand inundation, Newborough was a place of rich farmland that had a causeway out to the little ferry port on Aber Menai Point (D), and a once larger estuary down to Dwyran. Note that many modern maps still indicate the old causeway as a – non-existent and potentially dangerous – footpath out over the sands from Penlon parking site (E) to the point. Ongoing fears that dunes would swallow Newborough later prompted Tudor Queen Elizabeth I to legalise the protection of marram grass, still an essential part of stabilising the dunes. The tough grass also provided raw material for a prosperous industry: weaving the long spear-like leaves into mats, brooms and baskets.

The new extensive dunes nurtured another industry, hence the English name of Newborough Warren: European rabbits quickly colonized, with over 100,000 a year harvested for food at the peak. No doubt their predators also flourished (bearing in mind often indiscriminate 'predator control'). Well, all such interests, including gamekeeping, faded to some degree in the last century, with the 1950s

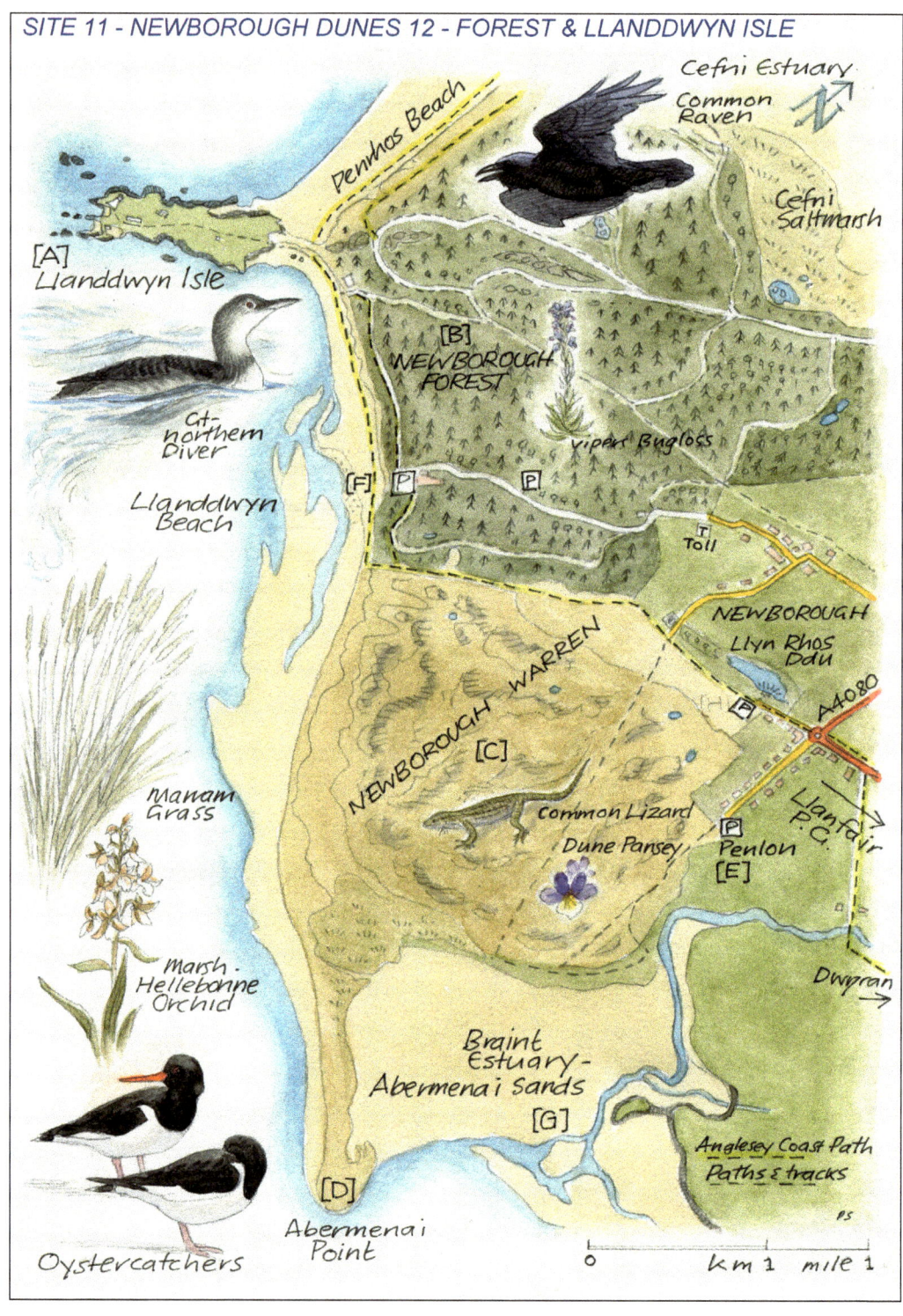

SITE 11 - NEWBOROUGH DUNES 12 - FOREST & LLANDDWYN ISLE

Penrhos Beach

Cefni Estuary

Common Raven

Cefni Saltmarsh

[A] Llanddwyn Isle

Gt. northern Diver

[B] NEWBOROUGH FOREST

Vipers Bugloss

[F] [P] [P]

Llanddwyn Beach

T Toll

NEWBOROUGH

Llyn Rhos Ddu

A4080

NEWBOROUGH WARREN

[C]

Marram Grass

Common Lizard

Dune Pansey

[H] [P]

Llanfair P.G.

[P] Penlon [E]

Marsh Helleborine Orchid

Dwyran

Braint Estuary - Abermenai Sands

[G]

Anglesey Coast Path

Paths & tracks

ps

[D]

Abermenai Point

0   km 1   mile 1

Oystercatchers

myxomatosis epidemic severely curtailing the rabbits, and establishment of forestry, resulting in changes to the dune vegetation – and hence the wildlife. The extensive belts of trees, largely conifers, were planted for both shelter from the perennially encroaching sands and as a commercial cash crop.

Yet the dunes still cover an extensive area and are recognised as an internationally important ecological site that is positively awash with acronyms – it's an SSSI, SAC, NNR and part of the AONB. The roughly three or four stages of most dunes, as at Aberffraw, support a very wide variety of F&F that have been adapted to survive in 'extreme' salty conditions, from very dry to very wet. Beginning with little 'embryonic' or 'fore-dunes' at the high tide mark, they reach back via 'mobile' to 'semi-fixed/fixed dunes', then wet 'humid dune slacks', before naturally climaxing in scrub, heath and finally scrub woodland at the rear, where winds are naturally more subdued. It is typically seen by the Braint Estuary on the Warren's south-east corner, now such trees are no longer removed.

On the dry outer fore and mobile dunes marram grass still dominates, although the rest of the sands are also vegetated by a whole range of interesting plants, which originally depended on wind-blown, open sand cover. We commonly find lots of tricolour dune pansies, with spikes of sea spurge, exotic sea holly and even the rare, lichen-like petalwort in the more open areas. Then there's the lovely little sand cat's tail and hare's-foot among the many typical grasses, like red fescue and sand bent. Between many of the dune hillocks, in the damp, flat marshy hollows or 'slacks', another rich flora can be found, including lots of creeping dune willow's tiny bushes, creeping dewberry, white-flowered grass of Parnassus, bright blue viper's bugloss and a wide variety of orchids including several spotted species, as well as bee, pyramidal, pale marsh and the even more spectacular marsh helleborine orchid (note the very similar broad-leaved helleborine in adjacent forest clearings, although I haven't seen any for decades). There's also lots of the not too dissimilar wintergreen, or a few 'carnivorous' plants like butterwort, and the equally parasitic – but on fungi, not flies! – yellow bird's-nest.

Fungi, typically, are dominated by slender parasols, field, horse and fairy ring mushrooms, 'dung fungi' like psilocybes, various wax-caps and the rare nail

Slender parasol mushroom, Aberffraw.

Slender Parasol mushroom, Aberffraw

fungus. Bryophytes like mosses and lichens commonly carpet or underpin large areas among other plants, such as 'Reindeer' and 'Homolothecium' mosses, although rarer thread mosses like sea bryum, as formerly at Aberffraw, are possibly still here with their rare petalwort kin.

Dunes also host numerous vertebrates, if not always obvious, from the usual mammals like red fox, otter, polecat, stoat, weasel, hedgehog, mole, field vole, field mouse, brown hare and European rabbit (some black) to the usual amphibians and reptiles. Common frogs and common toads, as well as various newts, are naturally found around the stock pools including the rare great crested or warty, as well as the pretty common newt and very widespread and smaller palmate newt, which is identified by its black, rear webbed feet. Adders and slow-worms are not uncommon, unlike sand lizards, which have been especially reintroduced here, if in small numbers, and are not to be confused with the very widespread, and usually much more somber-coloured, common lizard. The pools often have several interesting water plants and invertebrates like damselflies, including the common blue and beautiful demoiselle, and specialist dragonflies like hairy and little red darter. Where the pools still have steep sandy banks, sand martins can nest.

As for invertebrate insects there are, as virtually anywhere on earth, lots of them, including butterflies – up to twenty-four species such as the common, small blue, orange tip and dingy skipper – and several spectacular fritillaries like the small pearl-bordered or larger dark green. The many other insects include a huge variety of moths (although most are far more unobtrusive than the odd summer hummingbird hawkmoth), snails and slugs, many spiders, harvestmen, beetles, grasshoppers (such as common green or mottled), crickets (such as conehead), ladybirds, lacewings, hoverflies and other flies (including biting horseflies),

Palmate newts – adult 'tadpole' forms.

mosquitoes, (especially bird's nest) fleas, lice, ants, earwigs, woodlice and pill bugs, centipedes and millipedes, and wasps and bees, etc.. Some of the latter two are of the mining variety, thus favouring more open yet mildly compacted sands. This helps explain ongoing attempts by the NRW to create more open areas of sand, as elsewhere in Wales, although most dune systems in Europe are naturally drying out, quickly and naturally grassing over and vegetating. The dunes also need constantly grazing, currently here by Dexter and belted Galloway cattle, and, as with open parts of the forest, Welsh mountain ponies. These all encourage maritime and flowering plants and help control the taller, rank plants that smother them. Note that cattle, especially calves, can chase dogs, which are supposed to be on a lead here, in an effort to protect the very vulnerable, ground-nesting birds, flowers and plants.

Such birds include that essentially British songster the skylark, which still spiral heavenwards here alongside its much more modest mimic, the ubiquitous meadow pipit. Sadly, formerly common species like grey partridge, whinchat and cuckoo are now much more sporadic, although raven, common buzzard, kestrel, mistle thrush, wheatear, stonechat, sedge and grasshopper warbler, whitethroat, reed bunting and pied wagtail are still common enough, along with barn owl and the odd non-breeding short-eared owl and hen harrier. They are joined in winter by the secretive woodcock (via short evening flights from the forest) and even the odd lapwing, as on Aberffraw dunes, and possibly curlew, redshank or snipe, which can still breed. As with virtually every other site on Anglesey, commoner garden/woodland species like robin, dunnock, wren, blackbird, song thrush, siskin, chaffinch, goldfinch, blue and great tit, willow warbler, chiff-chaff and blackcap, collared dove, wood pigeon, carrion crow, jackdaw and magpie, etc., are also found around the forest and garden edges of the dunes. Sadly, yellowhammer or yellow bunting is another declining species, especially on this side of Môn, although an uncommon little bunting has wintered here, and the likes of Lapland and snow bunting, or water pipit, occasionally grace the shoreline flotsam and jetsam.

The more remote tidelines, as out on Abermenai Point, are now the last refuge of breeding ringed plover and oystercatchers, even with their incredibly well camouflaged ground nests – questing dogs and tramping feet, however careful, are now their biggest enemy. Ironically, the low tide shoreline right in front of the Forest car park (F) can host over a hundred brent geese in the winter, alongside the usual gulls and local carrion/hooded crow 'crosses'.

To the south-east, the wide sands of the Braint Estuary and Traeth Melynog (G) usually hold typical wildfowl and waders, in season, such as shelduck, mallard, wigeon, teal and pintail, red-breasted merganser or goldeneye, and redshank, curlew, ringer plover, knot and dunlin alongside considerable winter flocks of green (lapwing) and golden plover. Virtually any other wader can also be found here at various times, like the two godwits, mournful-sounding grey plover, the usual three sandpipers, greenshank, whimbrel, and, as always near water, grey heron and little egret. (Note that the normally abandoned practice of punt-gunning is still licensed at the river mouth on winter low tides, although the estuary, in a SAC, SSSI and AONB, is supposed to be a sanctuary between the two local shooting estuaries.)

The beaches here have long been famous for their cleanliness and sheer space, although the official Newborough Forest toll car park can get rather full in high summer, like the village (note other car parks at (E), or the nearby Malltraeth Cob (Site 10)).

Llyn Rhos-Ddu (H) is the biggest permanent pool, complete with its own bird hide, car park with distinctive yellow grass sculpture, and long access trails spraying out widely to forest, beach and dunes. The little lake itself has typical Anglesey waterbirds and water life, such as great crested and little grebes, tufted duck, coot, 'mere-hen', water rail and the usual geese, plus mute swans, sometimes joined in winter by whoopers. The beautiful, if poorly named, bogbean commonly grows on its margins, along with marsh marigold.

Traeth (Beach) Llanddwyn (F) is the most accessed beach, with amazing views across to Snowdonia and the Llŷn Peninsula. Traeth Penrhos, to the north, is just as attractive if far quieter, eventually leading around to the Cefni estuary, either via the long sandy shore, or dunes and forest when the weather is overly 'damp'. They are effectively separated by the lovely Ynys Llanddwyn (A) – an island in name only, apart from when very high spring tides cut it off (note spring tides usually occur in both spring and autumn). Its iconic little lighthouse and row of old pilot and lighthouse keepers' cottages, Tai Peilotiaid, should house an exhibition of local life in recent centuries – hence the recent *1900 Island* TV series. Its current popularity is both marred and enhanced by everything from the so-called reality TV shows and dubious films about Greek myth to our own 'Welsh St Valentine', St Dwynwen, the erstwhile 'patron saint of Welsh lovers'. The ruined church is where she is reputed to have retired to, as a nun, to lick her lovelorn wounds. The island has other wildlife that is also currently suffering from the sheer weight of visitors, yachts and water sports – and dogs, supposedly only on leads on the isle, and not allowed on much of Traeth Llanddwyn at all in the summer. A few grey seals are still seen here, though, even pupping nearby in the autumn, and great cormorant and shags still nest en masse on the islets with the three regular gull species, whereas formerly common ring plover and oystercatcher are virtually extinct as nesters on the island's little beaches. Meadow pipit, stonechat, skylark, wheatear, common raven and even chough all still nest on the ground or cliffs here, whereas the likes of waders such as purple sandpiper, turnstone and sanderling usually only grace the rocks and nearby shores in non-breeding seasons. Ironically, this is one of the few places to see common gulls among the usual Larus species, if largely winter.

Offshore, ragged black strings of common scoter ducks typically undulate above the waves at almost any season, although the many northern gannet, Manx shearwater and various tern species like sandwich and Arctic terns fishing here are largely a summer phenomena. Their almost constant diving for fry and sand eels attracts predatory Arctic or great skuas, especially on passage as many birds like our auks also move south. In the non-breeding season, massive great northern or daintier red-throated divers also dive for fish here, joining the smaller resident black guillemots, razorbills and various grebes, as detailed more at sites like Lynas Point (Site 38).

The island has many of the same plants, flowers, fungi and bryophyte species as seen on nearby heaths and cliffs, and is especially blessed with lots of bright pink (virtually impossible to digitally photograph or paint!) bloody cranesbill.

Above left: Bloody cranesbill.

Above right: Common lobster.

The rocks and cliffs are often coated with attractive lichens, from the commonest orange, Xanthoria and Caloplaca species usually at the top, or tufty grey-green Ramalinas, then whiteish ones down to a typically broad band of black Verrucarias along the tideline, just above the silvery barnacle zone exposed at low water. The rocky shore is also beset with many seaweeds, from large Laminaria kelp forests only seen at very low waters, through several bladder-wrack or wrack species, to variously smaller edible treats like traditional Welsh laver bread (Porphyra species), similar dulse or carrageen and bright green sea lettuce. Lobsters lurk here, too, if only seen at very low tides. As for other crustaceans or shellfish, if these beaches had as many live ones as shell remains, we would be buried under razor clams, common cockles and mussels, scallops, otter and sand gaper shells, sea urchins and even oysters, as well as more common winkles and whelks, or spider, shore and edible crab shells. Yet we rarely see many of them alive, like the many colourful tellins or even cowries found here as empty shells. We can also find thousands of fascinating sea gooseberries floating in the shallows in the summer, almost transparent bodies alive with pulsing fronds and looking not unlike miniature jellies – although non stinging.

Fish, of course, are also plentiful – if sometimes hard to catch on rod and line – and range from various shark (largely dogfish, now renamed as catshark, species) already mentioned to some of commonest inshore ones. These include various smaller, colourful cuckoo, rainbow or larger ballan wrasse, pollack and coalfish, rays, and well-camouflaged flatties like plaice and flounder. The presence of Atlantic bass, mackerel and scad, sea scorpion, garfish or bright lumpfish, little butterfish and pipefish, and fairly regular sightings of cetaceans like leaping bottle-nosed dolphins, means there is usually something to observe in the sea here, along with various jellyfish, moon jellies especially, but also large numbers of stinging, red-brown lion's mane jellyfish, and sometimes even Portuguese man-o'-war as recently washed up after gales. Although not common either, we have had spectacular, post-storm beaching of literally thousands of the little blue-sailed 'by-the-wind-sailor' jellies, although stranding of huge barrel jellies is more likely nowadays, if usually without the long tentacles of similar species.

As for the Geology Trail, noticeably extending out from the forest ridge onto the island, it's complex and already world-famous. With a mangled mix of the catastrophically laid basement of largely Pre-Cambrian rocks, including pillow lavas and a whole colourful, serpentine melange of pink, red, white, green, grey and blue limestones, volcanics and metamorphics, quartzites, jaspers, etc., it's basically a smaller version of the huge turbidite sedimentary fans that underpin most continents. It also produces superb rock pools. Although artfully plastered with pink coralline, red beadlet anemones, and brimming with crabs like shore, hermit and masked, common and brittle starfish, small fish like gobies and blennies, and plentiful prawns & shrimps, etc., the pools, sadly, are often at the foot of steep and dangerous rocks. The tiny 'black pepper-like' grains drifting across some pools, tardigrades or 'water bears', are one of the hardiest critters on earth, however hot or cold the environment.

Newborough Forest has rather a mixed rep nowadays as one of the best places to see red squirrels – or as an artificial destroyer of the dunes! Several authorities still want to fell most of the trees despite the woodland's popularity, especially since the successful reintroduction of the squirrels. Yes, the trees are 'artificial' in as much as they were only planted on the dunes post-war, for both cycling cash crop and protection of the area from encroaching sands, as they still do. Yet, more paradoxically, although the trees also help dry out the dunes, they have never been wetter than in recent decades, for the sands are cupped in underlying volcanic troughs and the forest itself has many springs radiating out from its central ridges, let alone heavier winter rain nowadays. However, ironically, the authorities actually need dry dunes for those scarce insects and bryophytes – hence artificially stripping dune vegetation and trees to enhance open sandy areas, although they quickly revegetate.

Yes, the dunes are a very important ecosystem, but the woods have become a great symbiotic sideshow, shared and used by many of the same creatures, if some prey on others. The trees also provide lots of different tracks for everyone from nature watcher, cycle and horse rider to runner and walker, and shelter from the wild Atlantic weather. The rapidity with which red squirrels have recolonised these largely 'foreign' pine trees and their vital cones (as also for our red crossbills or, to a lesser degree, great spotted woodpeckers), plus the huge common raven roost – until recently the second largest raven roost in the world – shows their importance. There is also the usual selection of garden/woodland birds, as already mentioned for the Warren Dunes, plus exotic jay, redpoll, nuthatch, treecreeper and occasional firecrest alongside the many goldcrests and general tit and finch flocks, or summer warblers. We also have regularly nest-prospecting ospreys (amongst other racy raptors like sparrowhawk and goshawk), attracted doubtless by the three great local estuaries.

The forest has much more F&F to enjoy, though, especially in more mature parts, regenerating clear felled areas or horse-grazed slacks. With the pools, this means a whole variety of water life, as already described for the dunes, plus the rare medicinal leech. One thing we have largely lost, though, as when any conifer plantation matures, are open areas of vegetation like ling heather and bilberry around the young trees, hence also birds like whinchat, tree pipit and nightjar. In Newborough's case, exceptionally, the young trees harboured rare breeding Montagu's and hen harriers, short-eared owls and merlin. However, trees grow rapidly, and by the late 1960s the birds were largely gone as the canopy inevitably closed (see Tunnicliffe's *Shorelands Summer Diary*). Mind you, the elegant Monty's breeding range in Britain has generally retreated anyway.

Yet it is not all conifers, as many parts have a rich understory or whole areas of important, berried, nutted or seeded trees like wild cherry, cotoneaster, hazel, alder and birch, with blackberries galore (I recently saw a rare hummingbird hawkmoth on the berries (August 2019)). There are exotic trees too, like the medicinal-smelling balsam poplar, white poplar, or many smaller willows and hawthorn, sometimes swathed with butterfly and moth-loving old man's beard, or honeysuckle. Mammals typically include many of those included for the Dunes – plus possibly badger – but as for bats, of the seven possible on Môn, the most likely here are brown long-eared and the two pipistrelles, with noctule bat at least seen nearby. Appropriately, the forest has dozens of bat boxes, told by little metal discs (if many need repairing). Reptiles and amphibians are also the same as for the dunes, or the many ponds, ditches and slacks in and around the forest, including newts of the usual three species and lots of common frog spawn – unless killed by late frosts or, conversely, drying out.

As for insects, dragonflies and damselflies are particularly common in the clearings and rides in summer, dominated by many bright common/red darters (note females are far duller) and common blue damselflies, with the striking blue and yellow-green southern hawker, emperor or large ringed dragonfly occasionally demonstrating their aerobatic skills. Likewise butterflies, although the brown speckled wood and ringlets are usually the commonest, and dingy skipper one of the rarest. Of the many other insects, the large conifer needle nests of 'red' wood ants are notable, with sometimes considerable numbers of honey bees, hoverflies, the odd bee fly, plumes of winter gnats and much more.

Then there's the varied plant life most insects depend on, including many pretty wild flowers, beginning with early snowdrops, lesser celandine and bluebells. Many that follow are quite large, like the blue or yellow spikes of viper's bugloss and evening primrose that line many tracks, alongside pink foxglove, fireweed (willowherb sps), red campion and purple loosestrife, or the many ox-eye daisies, umbellifers, knapweeds, docks, etc., sometimes draped with skeins of white bellbine. On a smaller scale and usually in clearings, we commonly find yellow silverweed and bird's-foot trefoil, or purple tufted vetch, among large carpets of wintergreen, orchids, and far too many other plants to mention here. The uncommon shore dock growing in damp spots deserves a mention though, as the rare if very close kin of the common dock. Hence some ditches are especially dammed, also to bring the general water table up for the dunes – when they want them wet, not dry, that is.

The trees nourish a very rich array of lichens, mosses, and fungi, too, if the latter are usually dominated by yellow 'Slippery Jack' boletus, or several pink or purple

Newborough fungi.

russulas that take some sorting. Then there's that witchy favourite, the bright red and white spotted fly agaric, or lots of saffron milk caps. Fungi comes in scores of shapes and sizes, from what looks like bright yellow foam, or butter, over to the black balls of King Alfred's cakes, fleshy pink wood ears, or exquisite little umbrellas of fairy caps. Several of the boletus/Suillus, with vertical instead of horizontal tube gills, are also here, such as the elegant birch bark boletus and 'Cep' (boletus edulis), with lots of brackets, polypores, honey and sulphur tufts, and even the odd death cap or false death cap – do be careful with fungi. I wouldn't even advise sniffing some, as spores are often loose, and expert-led fungi forays are available here at Llyn Parc Mawr or over at Treborth Botanical Gardens by Menai Bridge.

Below such exotic fruiting bodies – as the main part of the fungi is that massive world-wide-web of hyphae threads – we often have a much more subtle world, of subtly hued carpets of mosses, with hard fern and dry Cladonia 'reindeer' lichens (the latter now less famed as model railway trees than as entrées in pricey restaurants). They especially flourish in open, drier areas, which also have lots of 'mini-blackberries', or dewberries, or, more rarely, bilberry, among small patches of heathers. Most ferns naturally prefer damper, darker or rockier places, and typically these woods have many hart's-tongue and large royal ferns.

Just across the main A4080 road from the main forest, with its own car park, Llyn Park Mawr Community Woodland (see Malltraeth map) is one of the best places to see red squirrels in Wales – should the car park be reasonably quiet. Many folks sit in their car and watch and photograph them on the feeders, although they can be seen virtually anywhere in the forest. Its pool attracts otters and even the occasional osprey, although you are much more liable to see breeding and wintering waterbirds like little grebes, gadwall, tufted duck, shoveller, coot and 'mere-hen', or the odd wigeon, oystercatcher and the usual geese. Little egrets roost here, too, and red foxes regularly patrol the margins at dusk, while brown hares are a bit of a speciality of surrounding fields, like barn owls and winter woodcock. Replacement hides, long promised, should provide an even better viewing experience.

So, all in all, the forest is both a great place to nature watch and walk in, or see and access the many wonderful surrounding landscapes. Walking its central rocky valley in a cold, winter dusk, listening to the eerily echoing raven conversation, or awakening woodcock, is one of Môn's top birdy attractions, but then so is exploring virtually anywhere in this glorious area of sea, shore, woodland and dune.

Once the Coast Path leaves Newborough Warren, it briefly follows the A4080 past the famed Marram Grass Restaurant, before diverting back towards the coast. It crosses the little Afon Braint estuary by a unique set of very large stepping stones – not for the short of step – before meandering either inland to Dwyran, or back to the Strait and eastwards to Foel Ferry. The area is generally good for barn owl, winter woodcock, and the usual seasonal farmland birds and assorted F&F.

SSSI, SAC, AONB, NRW, Geo-Môn

Site 13: Cors Ddyga RSPB Reserve
OS reference SH 464-725

This is the third RSPB reserve on the island, and newest, but by no means the least. As already covered at Malltraeth (Site 10), this almost entirely island-splitting marsh was damned 200 years ago to claim land for coal mining and farming. Draining was augmented by embanking the formerly meandering Afon Cefni and adding two independent side channels and lots of adjacent ditches, gradually creating small fields and settlements, like Paradwys (B). Another important construction that quickly followed was Telford's Menai Suspension Bridge, thereby permanently converting Anglesey from an island and enabling the establishment of Holyhead's important Irish ferry port, and furthering the prodigious exports from Amlwch's 'Copper Mountain' (Site 41). The London–Holyhead A5 traversing the marsh followed, as the A55 expressway now also crosses here. Formerly, the main route from Holyhead to the mainland was via the Strait at Beaumaris, effectively bypassing the large mire. The RSPB reserve now covers this part of the damp vale, long known as Cors Ddyga, or 'Tygai's Marsh', named after a sixth-century Breton Christian monk who came to this remote wetland to establish a church in the historical Arthur's tumultuous times. The remains of the nineteenth-century Pentre Berw coal mine can at least still be seen here, via a new, shorter marsh trail and sculpture feature by the chimney and ruins (C), or in some of the now wildlife-rich lakes, which resulted from collapsed mine workings.

Nowadays, mining coals or souls is not the remit, but saving rare wetland birds like bittern, marsh harrier and lapwing, or uncommon water voles, aquatic plants, beetles and dragonflies, etc. Various organisations are ably assisting RSPB Cymru

SITE 13 - CORS DDYGA RSPB RESERVE

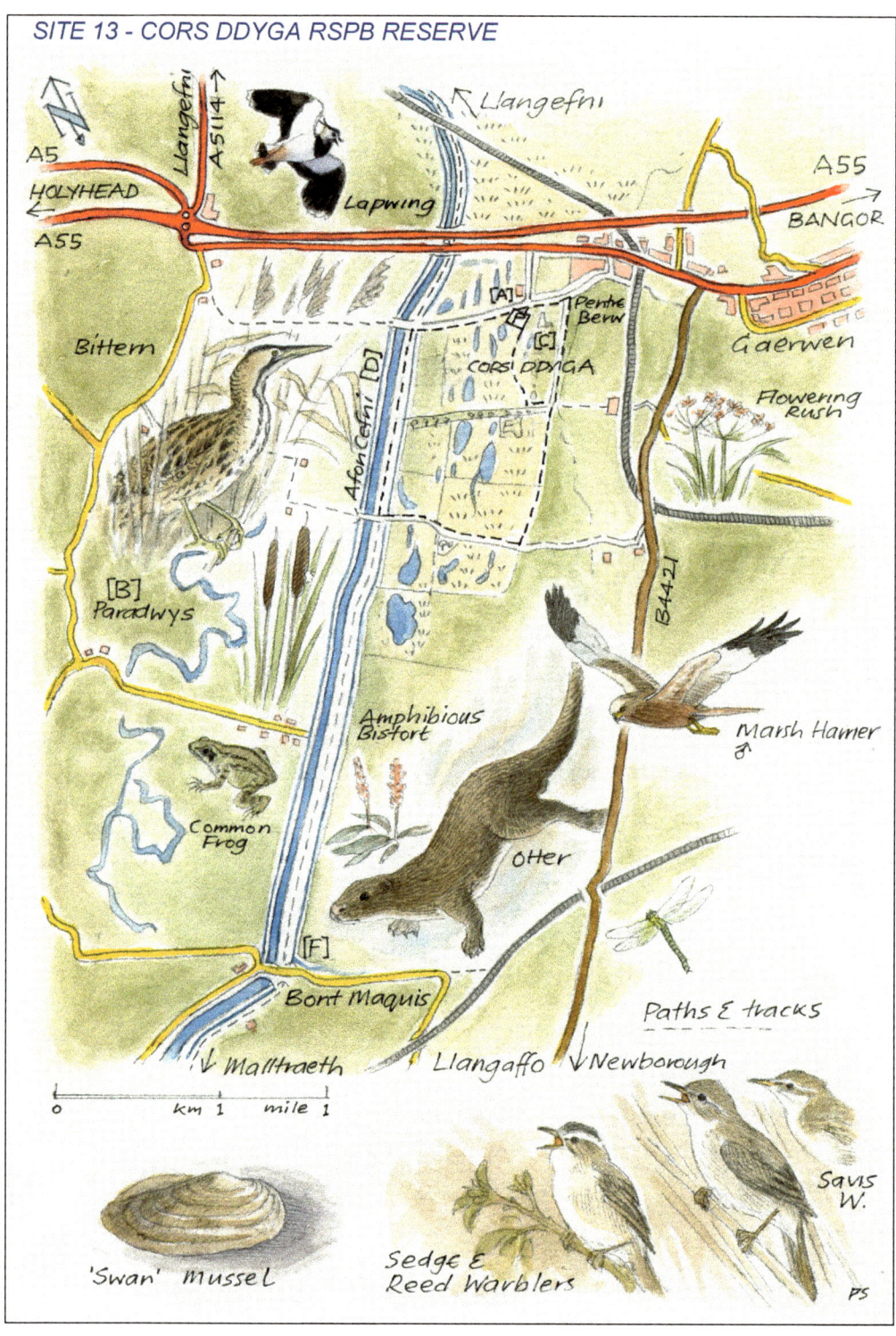

A5
HOLYHEAD
A55

Llangefni
A5114 →

↑ Llangefni

Lapwing

A55
→ BANGOR

Gaerwen

[A]
Pentre Berw
[C]
CORS DDYGA

Bittern

Flowering Rush

Afon Cefni [D]

[B]
Paradwys

Marsh Harrier ♂

Amphibious Bistort

B4421

Common Frog

Otter

[F]
Bont Maquis

Paths & tracks

↓ Malltraeth

Llangaffo

↓ Newborough

0   km 1   mile 1

Savi's W.

'Swan' Mussel

Sedge & Reed Warblers

PS

in this, like the Heritage Lottery Fund, the Gaynor Cemlyn-Jones Trust and the Welsh Governments Sustainable Development Fund, as it lies in the local AONB.

It has taken many years to get the marsh back up to scratch for wildlife, involving planting lots of common reed and allies, digging new pools and scrapes, and raising water levels where needed. The newish cycle track alongside the Afon Cefni (D) ensures wheelchair access, while an existing network of tracks and paths cover most of the rest, although there are no hides there yet (2019), and car parking is mainly at (A) by the RSPB offices. Some tracks can also be very wet at times, but that's the point, for as is so often the case, once a marsh habitat is renewed, the birds and other life return – toot sweet. Neither bittern nor marsh harrier has bred on Anglesey for forty or so years, but have now nested here every year since at least 2015. Yet just as important are the lapwing, curlew, common snipe, shoveller, skylark, Cetti's and reed warblers, stonechat, whinchat, sand martin, barn owl and kingfisher. As are water vole and otter, flowering rush, nationally scarce hairy dragonfly and blue-tailed damselfly, or the rare water beetles that also thrive here. That is largely because many are protected by large reed beds or even miles of fox-proof electric fencing in the case of the lapwing. Or by building banks of nest pipes on the Afon Cefni for sand martins, and putting up nest boxes for barn owls and kestrels. Other typical wetland birds are increasingly dropping in, or wintering, like the 2017 autumn flock of forty-two ruff, or thirty plus black-tailed godwits, both of which have lingered into summer and will possibly soon breed. The usual Môn diving ducks – tufted duck and pochard – plus the omnipresent mallard and two resident geese species, shoveller, gadwall, shelduck, mute swan, and great crested and little grebes, which all live and breed here, although they are often hard to observe on the largely reed-fringed lakes, pools and ditches.

Meadow pipits are one of the commonest birds observed, winter or summer, and their exuberant song flight is superficially like the skylark's, if shorter and less melodious, but both have been joined by exciting new sounds here in recent springs. Evening is usually the best time to hear the weird buzzing or 'drumming' of the common snipes two vibrating outer tail feathers as it undulates above the damp fields, but the even stranger, eerie 'booming' call of the bittern is harder to pin down. Like corncrakes, which nested here until the 1960s – and might well again – they often appear to be throwing their voices over vast distances. Cetti's warblers are another new and particularly loud addition to the reedy chorus, supplemented by the various chattering and rattling of sedge, reed and grasshopper warblers in summer, or the typical year-round marsh-side reed buntings. Now (2019) we also have the first ever Savi's warblers to nest in Wales joining them, although their weird whirring song is unfortunately like the similar grasshopper warbler, all but inaudible to old ears like mine. On the debit side, although stonechats are still widespread on Anglesey, migrant whinchats are nothing like as common as they used to be, and only the odd pair breed here.

Not so with marsh harriers, another welcome returnee, especially when males (largely) do their superb undulating *'sky dance'* over the reeds, or birds of all ages slowly and elegantly quarter the marsh on typically upraised wings. Note they have hugely varying plumages, juveniles usually starting off dark chocolate with varying amounts of cream or ginger on crown and chin, with females gradually adding larger creamy patches to their forewing, breast and underwing, year by year. Males likewise get lighter with age, but with large pale grey wing patches

Marsh harrier and red kite.

and tails increasingly contrasting with their reddish or creamy bodies (generally speaking). With so much avian, mammalian, amphibian, reptilian and insect prey, other aerial predators include up to three pairs of nesting barn owls, sparrowhawk, common buzzard and tawny owl, while one or two hen harriers currently join their marsh cousins here in winter. Naturally, our most glamorous and aerobatic raptors, resident peregrine and wintering merlin falcons, even red kites also hunt here, especially with the modest winter starling roost, and small flocks of fieldfare and redwing enjoying the many hawthorn berries and assorted hips and haws. Finches, too, often gather here after breeding, like late summer flocks of goldfinches and linnets, or small parties of bullfinches, all lovers of weeds like the assorted thistle, umbellifer, cranesbill, plantain and dock species. Wood pigeons, common ravens and jays are also surprisingly common, especially around the central 'Oak Avenue' (E), which opens onto several other good marsh viewing areas.

Other small birds include varying numbers of resident pied wagtails, among good numbers of spring white wagtails, or the summer swifts, swallows, house martins and (usually) breeding sand martins that all hunt over the marsh and pools. Those dragonfly and hirundine specialists, hobbies, make brief summer visits, as elsewhere on Anglesey and Wales generally. As for other waterbirds, a small flock of winter whooper swans and half a dozen Greenland white-fronted geese have recently joined the resident geese and mute swans, with the white-fronts also sometimes on the wet farm stock fields nearer Bont Marquis (F). That was also the 2017–18 winter hotspot for half a dozen cattle egrets, although note that little egrets also follow stock animals in the damp, ox-bowed fields around Paradwys. In addition, we have a partial albino greylag goose with a white face, looking superficially like a white-fronted goose, let alone the genuine 'blue' snow geese currently here. With the increasing presence of great white egret here, plus purple heron and spoonbill, the odd glossy ibis, squacco and night heron, and sporadic breeding spotted and even Baillon's crakes, we just need the promised Mediterranean weather, too. Not that that won't also affect other life, but climate change is nothing new.

Brown hares are usually the most prominent mammal here, although otters and their families are regularly seen in the side channels even by the busy cycle track, and red fox, stoat, weasel, and doubtless the nocturnal polecat all hunt too. Mole and hedgehog in their own little ways as well, although both are eaten by common buzzard and other predators. Largely thanks to the ongoing Water Vole Project, one of their greatest enemies, American mink, are slowly being eradicated, as witnessed by many floating platforms of mink rafts, which monitor before later trapping them. Water shrews, which are larger and darker than common shrews, are also present with their usual kin, although more nocturnal and sometimes only seen in owl pellets. There are many other common rodents, such as brown rat, short-tailed and bank voles, or the three usual mice species (although harvest mouse is another possibility, known only from heathland sites by Llangoed, I think). As bats are often found by water, a rich source of insects, the marsh is no exception, with the usual pipistrelles and brown long-eared, and less common noctule or even lesser horseshoe bat, and probably Daubenton's.

With so much water we expect the usual rich assortment of amphibians such as common frog and common toad, and all three regular newt species including the rarer great crested. Fish too, of course, if supposedly still restricted to rudd, common eels and three-spined stickleback. Certainly, large numbers of fish fry dimple the pools in summer, probably chased by larger ones and providing prime food for resident kingfisher, little egret, great crested and little grebes. Very noticeable shoals of summer breeding grey mullet penetrate as far upriver as here, as do flatties, silvery sea trout and even the odd Atlantic salmon. As for reptiles, I have seen just one young grass snake here – dangling from a marsh harriers claws! Then there's the slow-worm I watched a grey heron slowly shaking into submission, or the half-swallowed adder carried off by a common buzzard. Such sightings can be, perversely, good news for the populations of many species, like the common lizard's tails that are deliberately discarded during predator attacks. Or the large number of dead badgers, even otters and polecats, on North Wales roads, as with red squirrels and brown hares on Anglesey. There are also plentiful freshwater or swan mussels here, as evidenced by large, broken shells regularly that are seen on the tracks – probably discarded by otters, grey herons or corvids.

Finally, insects and plants, another interdependent and very rich biotope here. Some of the most noticeable are the dragonflies, with eleven species recorded, three of which are nationally scarce, as already mentioned, among others like the black-tailed skimmer, variable damselfly, hawkers like the golden-ringed and emperor, and a new resident, the southern hawker (identified by its bright neon-green eyes). Darters, too, such as the powder blue male or gold female,

Broad-bodied chaser.

broad-bodied chaser and common/red darter, are fairly common, plus the gorgeous banded demoiselle damselfly. Butterflies and moths are also fairly plentiful, consisting of the usual species, although especially favoured by red admiral and peacock, and when 'irrupting' from Europe masses of painted ladies. Cockchafers – and possibly glow-worms by the drier margins – are sometimes seen, although the north and east of the island seems better for the latter bioluminescers. Some of the water beetles are also special, if rather specialist – such as *Loccobuis sinuatus* and *Rhantus grapii* – yet one of the commonest here is the largest and snappiest, great diving beetle, often seen crawling across paths. Yes, it can bite. Like its sinuous, surface-hanging larvae, or the many dragonfly and damselfly larvae that populate these waters, often feeding on small fish and tadpoles. Yet there is a whole array of pond life just waiting to be discovered by dipping here (with the RSPB), from water spiders with their amazing silvery diving bells to water boatmen and freshwater shrimps.

Common reed, or phragmites, is, as usual with most British wetlands, the most widespread and important water plant here, forming the dense reed beds so beloved of bittern, marsh harrier and reed warbler for both feeding and breeding (and cleansing and filtering waters). Hopefully, beautiful bearded reedlings are due to return since last breeding here following the very hard winter of 1963 that drove some west. They have recently reached Burton Mere on the Wirral, and have been seen at RSPB Conwy. Bulrush or reed mace, reed canary grass and branched bur reed, as well as the locally important reed sweet grass (looking like a slightly smaller, more elegant phragmites), make up most of the rest. The shallower and boggy areas have yellow flag iris, marsh marigold, juncus rush species, and the nationally scarce and tiny pillwort, which have been especially nurtured here. The lovely little pink or white spikes of amphibious bistort and bogbean are reasonably common on open water in summer, whereas the delicate pink flower heads of flowering rush are less so, if still spreading out along the many ditches. Horned pondweed, water violet, mare's tail, marsh stitchwort and autumnal starwort are other standout plants for the specialist. Note the use of lots of horses – including bijou Shetland ponies – for grazing here, with cows on other parts of the reserve, plus late summer cutting of some meadows, depending on season and desired plant control. In other words, a certain amount of grazing or cropping of the larger or denser plants is essential in maintaining smaller plants and flowers, and enough grassy, open areas for birds and other life to breed and feed. The success of some seventy pairs of nesting lapwings in recent years shows the wisdom of that, and attracting more and more specialists like great white egret, red kite, black-tailed godwit and ruff, or more water voles, dragonflies and various plants, with doubtless others still to come or revive.

From the RSPB marsh, the cycle track continues along the river either inland to Llangefni, under the A55, along often overgrown kingfisher territory, or westwards to Malltraeth, via the distinctive stone humpback bridge of Pont Maquis. A rough track along the south-east bank of the river passes the 'Big Bend' (Site 10), so beloved of greenshank, or goosander and red-breasted merganser families, and on the north bank reed and sedge warblers breed near the railway viaduct. Both banks are good for fungi like parasol and field/horse mushrooms, and puffball species both small and large – sometimes huge. You can also just make out a small lake at Glantraeth, home to typical waterbirds and and passed by a sometimes difficult footpath from Malltraeth to Paradwys. The fields often hold flocks of geese, sometimes with a couple of barnacle geese, or the odd pink foot. Cattle egrets have wintered between here and Pont Maquis, and birds from barn owl to kingfisher are regular.

RSPB, SSSI, GAT

SITE 14: PLAS NEWYDD, PORTHAMEL WOODS
OS Reference SH 520-695, 508-680

Plas Newydd (A) is the famed stately home of Lord and Lady Anglesey, on the Menai Strait, administered by the NT (National Trust) and also well known for its gardens – and red squirrels thanks to a recent reintroduction. Its often eccentric but absorbing history, archaeology, architecture, Whistler mural, exhibitions, water sports, rhododendron garden, tearoom and commanding position on the Menai Strait, yet surrounded with ample woodland and gardens, means there is something for everyone here. The gardens are both 'wild' and cultivated enough to enable a decent selection of typical Môn garden/woodland birds among the goodly collection of trees, both native and introduced. Smaller birds include the usual tits and finches, as well as summer visitors like chiff-chaff, willow and garden warbler, and blackcap. Year-round, tawny owl, sparrowhawk, common buzzard, pheasant, jay, nuthatch, treecreeper, great spotted and even green woodpecker (sadly otherwise still in decline on the island) are all likely. Similarly, the spotted flycatcher is another formerly common garden and woodland bird hereabouts, if only a summer visitor. On the positive side, the NT notes that the abandoned rugby pitch here has recently hosted up to '150,000 rare orchids'.

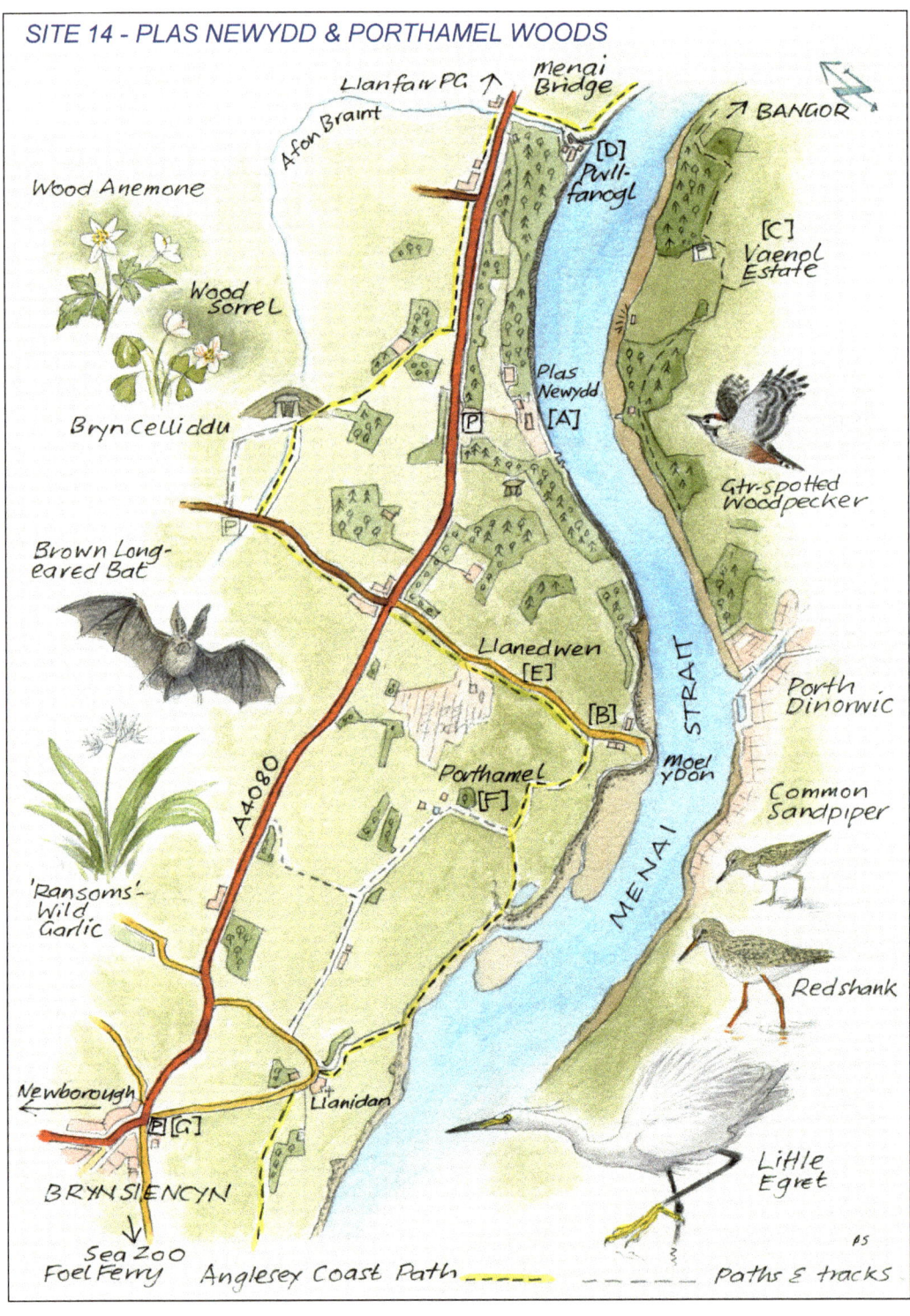

SITE 14 - PLAS NEWYDD & PORTHAMEL WOODS

Llanfair PG.
Menai Bridge
Afon Braint
BANGOR
[D]
Pwll-fanogl
Wood Anemone
[C]
Vaenol Estate
Wood Sorrel
Plas Newydd [A]
Bryn Celliddu
Gtr-spotted Woodpecker
Brown Long-eared Bat
Llanedwen [E]
[B]
Porth Dinorwic
A4080
Moel y Don
MENAI STRAIT
Common Sandpiper
Porthamel [F]
'Ransoms' Wild Garlic
Redshank
Newborough
Llanidan
BRYN SIENCYN
Little Egret
Sea Zoo Foel Ferry   Anglesey Coast Path _ _ _ _   _ _ _ _ Paths & tracks

The Strait itself was finally and rapidly cut via a large fault in the mixed bedrock sometime at the end of the Ice Age, although now also overlain with later sedimentary deposits. These can be seen particularly at the north-eastern, wider end, or in the masses of shifting sand banks down by Caernarfon. Yet there are lots of holes, gullies, reefs, boulders and coarse sediment and sand under the rushing waters, which, with the many eddies and other tidal movements, ensures a very rich marine environment. Hopefully, it will soon join our other few Marine Protected Areas (MPA). By the way, don't be taken in by the myth that the waters of the Strait merely drift back and forth with the tides, never properly flushing; they change almost completely every few days.

Hence the Menai Strait is of variable depth but still very fast here, so not that exceptional for birds. Most will be water fowl, with even the likes of winter great northern diver, and even the odd black- or red-throated, or great crested and little grebes, joining the great cormorants, shags and red-breasted mergansers that regularly dive in the jade-green currents. Summer terns also dance over the eddies, mainly common as used to breed near here, along with the sandwich terns, which seem to turn up everywhere, especially before and after dispersing from breeding areas like Cemlyn (Site 46). There is a busy grey heronry nearby, towards Moel-y-Don (B), now inevitably also stuffed with the little egrets that busily stalk every shore like slender white marionettes. Inevitably, there are comparatively few non-diving wildfowl and waders around such turgid waters. Yet shelduck, wigeon, teal, oystercatcher, curlew, both godwits, redshank, whimbrel, turnstone, dunlin, green, grey and golden plover, and common and green sandpipers can all be found at one time or another, especially on the open or muddy bits westwards towards Foel Ferry. Incidentally, there is also a good view of the Strait and Plas Newydd from the opposite shore, on the Vaenol Estate (C), via a little NT car park near Parc Menai by Britannia Bridge.

Although mainly freshwater river birds (grey wagtail, dipper and kingfisher) all use the Strait, where such waterways as the little Afon Braint (D) – one of the few rivers to exit at two separate places – enter. Likewise by the Afon Cadnant (Site 16), possibly Afon Lleiniog (Site 21), and certainly by the larger Afon Ogwen on the other shore, by Penrhyn Castle and the wonderful Aber Ogwen/Spinnies NWWT Reserve.

Even bottle-nosed dolphins can occasionally cavort in pods here and the odd grey seal – or, by Bangor Pier recently, the even rarer common seal. The waters themselves are well known for their rich marine life, with many fish, from Atlantic bass to tope, grey mullet to catsharks, conger eel, cod, whiting and pouting, or colourful little wrasse species like rainbow, to lots of whitebait (Site 15). Little sea slugs and sea hares of varying colours and exotic patterns are also found, as around much of the coast, like the octopi and even cuttlefish and squid species. Algae in the form of many very different seaweeds abounds, and as for corals, sponges, bryozoans, molluscs and marine worms and the like, we are more than well supplied with such encrusting life. Even crabs can wear 'designer suits' of small orange sponges. The encrusters range from the large, extravagant plumose anemones, as on some pier supports, to white, spooky-looking 'dead man's fingers' deeper down, and many more exotic-looking sponges, or sea squirts and hydroids (jelly-like critters). Not that they get much more bizarre than sea spiders, or the bioluminescent noctiluca plankton sometimes seen stranded, still flashing when disturbed. Such abundant sea life such as other phytoplankton are not so welcome, though, as when 'blooming', they can discolour and choke large areas of sea, and even smother shore life if washed up en masse.

Note that the Coast Path has to go inland from Llanedwen (E) then back alongside the main road from near Plas Newydd to Pwllfanog, just before Llanfairpwllgwyn. It continues along the Strait into Menai Bridge itself (Site 15).

The little woodland reserve of Porthamel (F) nestles at the heart of an interesting web of lanes, tracks, field and beach walks, from Moel-y-Don to Foel Ferry and the Sea Zoo at the extreme western end. There are several good vantage points for the various waterbirds and grey seals, fishing or loafing out on the shifting sand bars, and many stretches of stony shore commonly have typical limestone fossils, like shells and corals (see especially Penmon (Site 25)).

There's also access and parking at Brynsiencyn, by the new information café and pub (G). From there, well-vegetated and odiferous lanes (lots of wild garlic in spring!) lead down to the Strait by the very interesting old church and hall of Plas Llanidan (sometimes open to the public). The Coast Path also bears back west over fields steeped in history, seemingly where Romans crossed to decimate Druids. Closeness to the large Roman remains of Segontium, by Caernarfon, and lots of Roman metal artefacts already excavated here certainly support the theory. The Coast Path eastwards also splits here, either going along the shore at low tide, or slightly inland on a pleasant little lane among sheltering hedges, copses, woods, crops and fields more reminiscent of England than Môn. Hence slightly different birds, as one of the few places on the island to host lesser whitethroat, brambling (among winter finch flocks), grey partridge, yellowhammer and tree sparrow, although the latter trio are unpredictable nowadays.

As for the Coed Porthamel NWWT reserve itself, which the lane leads to, unfortunately access is currently (December 2019) not available or advised, as the little wood has considerable amounts of dumped rubbish, barbed wire and pitfalls (so often the lot of anywhere that has an old (limestone) quarry and abuts several farms). It is a great pity, as this peaceful, out-of-the-way location, despite being relatively small, has decent F&F – even formerly hosting nightingale, according to the NWWT blurb. Most of the birds are far more predictable, though, including common buzzard, sparrowhawk, tawny owl, wood pigeon and the odd stock dove, collared dove, great spotted woodpecker, nuthatch, treecreeper, jay and magpie. Of the smaller birds, summer visitors like blackcap, chiff-chaff, willow and garden warbler stand out among the usual tits, including long-tailed and coal tit and goldcrest, with the odd winter firecrest shining in the arboreal gloom. By the way, if you are ever going to find one of our very few Anglesey lesser-spotted woodpeckers, this might be the area for it. Otherwise I have only ever seen them in little woods by Pentraeth, Beaumaris, or over at the Spinnies.

Seasonally, the typical farmland all around will also have swallow, house martin, swift, lots of loafing or feeding gulls, common raven, carrion crow and rook, mixed finch or winter thrush gatherings (redwing, fieldfare, blackbird, mistle and song thrush), pied wagtails, or groups or individual of waders like lapwing, golden plover, curlew, oystercatcher, and lesser numbers of redshank and snipe. The Strait hereabouts, and especially down to Foel Ferry, can have unusual waterfowl like the neat little black-necked grebe, if usually in black and white winter dress, or when storm-bound, even northern gannet, Manx shearwater, storm petrel and black tern.

Coal, blue, great and long-tailed tits.

Porthamel's flowers can at least be seen from the lane, as well as large swathes of lesser celandine, wood sorrel, wood anemone, dog mercury, bluebell and the aforementioned wild garlic. Many trees are wrapped in ivy, or draped, like the limestone outcrops, with various mosses and hart's tongue fern. Naturally, the flora is dominated by lime-loving plants, like the ubiquitous ox-eye daisy, dead-nettle species, salad burnet, and various common spotted orchid varieties. Although somewhat untidy, the trees do contain some fine oaks, lots of ash, and beech, birch, field maple, the unusual hornbeam – beloved of hawfinches, although rarely seen on Môn – and a few statuesque Scots pine. Many fungi are also claimed, and the surrounding fields often harbour common species like horse and field mushroom, giant and small puffball, and I would guess the damp woodland might have species like smelly stinkhorn, strange witches jelly or scaly earth balls?

As for mammals, reptiles and amphibians, various bats are its main claim to fame, with the larger, paler noctule, the water-loving Daubenton's bat (small pools nearby) and the usual two tiny species of pipistrelles or brown long-eared. Such typical farmland with a lot of cover and hedges is also ideal for red fox, European rabbit, brown hare, stoat, weasel, polecat, hedgehog, mole, and the usual voles, mice and shrews. I have little doubt that common frogs, toads and various newts will be here somewhere, along with slow-worm and common lizard. As for insects, the wood's best shot is the exotic-sounding lesser-stag beetle, although claims for the much larger stags of various deer here are just as hard to establish, given the current closure of the wood. There are few deer on Môn, mainly fallow and largely confined to private estates.

Finally, the charming little harbour of Pwllfanog (D) that the Coast Path passes is well worth a mention. It was also the home of renowned Welsh artist Kyffin Williams RA OBE, a good friend of fellow academician, countryside painter and book illustrator C. F. Tunnicliffe. One of Kyffin's birdy highlights was nine great northern divers scooting past in an orderly line, following a typical, south-westerly winter gale.

NT, NWWT, MPA

SITE 15: COED CYRNOL WOODLAND AND MENAI BRIDGE
OS reference SH 554-716

Once the Coast Path passes Pwllfanog, it hugs a rocky bit of Strait famous for a large statue of Admiral Lord Nelson – although originally planned for Neptune – before passing under the massive stone pylons of Robert Stephenson's Britannia Bridge (B). The complex area between the two bridges is particularly rich in striking scenery, history and attendant wildlife, commonly viewed from the large lay-by and information area (A). Its famous scene of Telford's Menai Suspension Bridge, Church Island and Snowdonia must be one of the most photographed and painted in Wales. With sloping foreground fields, mixed woodland falling down to the rocky shore, and aerial view of the little Ynys Gorad Gôch island, with its distinctive harbour, white house and tower, it's certainly hard to beat. The Strait is also well known for jade-green waters, no doubt seeming even greener with the reflected summer woodlands and seasonal increase in phytoplankton. Yet this particular stretch is also notorious for the dangerous and unpredictable boils and eddies of the 'Swellies' and 'Platters' rocks, and especially the sinking of HMS *Conwy*, the Royal Naval training ship, in 1953. Fishermen ancient and modern love this area though, as the several historic fish traps or weirs on the northern shore, by Church Island (C), indicate, or the many rods and lines that can be seen nowadays. Incidentally, the tiny, well vegetated islet next to it is where little egrets first bred, with grey herons, in north-west Wales (though the main heronry is on the opposite shore, in Treborth Botanical Gardens, which is also well worth a visit for a rich collection of plants, fungi, and red squirrels).

The many birds here include all the usual gull species and summer terns such as the common terns, which used to breed on Ynys Gorad Gôch, and passing sandwich. The surrounding fields and shallows have the usual greylag and Canada geese, along with mute swan, shelduck, winter brent geese, wigeon, and ubiquitous mallard, all feeding on the various seagrasses and algae. The assorted diving birds include great crested and little grebe, great cormorant, shag, red-breasted merganser, goldeneye, the odd black guillemot and even common eider, and rarer scaup, or the odd black-throated and other divers. Waders like oystercatcher, curlew, whimbrel, redshank, spotted redshank, greenshank, grey plover, green (lapwing) and golden plover, dunlin and common and green sandpiper can all be seen along the shores during various seasons, or, where appropriate, flocking on the fields. There is a small hide just before the Coast Path heads up to the main road and into Menai Bridge, or down past Church Island.

Coed Cyrnol LNR (Local Nature Reserve) (D) is the first woodland you then come to, and considering its close proximity to bustling Menai Bridge is very well sited on the Strait, and leads down to the (wheelchair-friendly) Belgium Promenade under the suspension bridge and on into town. It's three separate, undulating woodlands in one – Coed Marquis, Coed Cyrnol and Coed yr Orsedd – interspersed with dramatic rocky outcrops and elegant Scots pine. It was also formerly a lookout or fort, hence Bronze Age artefacts being found. Nearer our times, Lord Henry Paget overlooks even Nelson from his dizzying Marquis of Anglesey Column up behind the other bridge. Sadly, it's no longer possible to

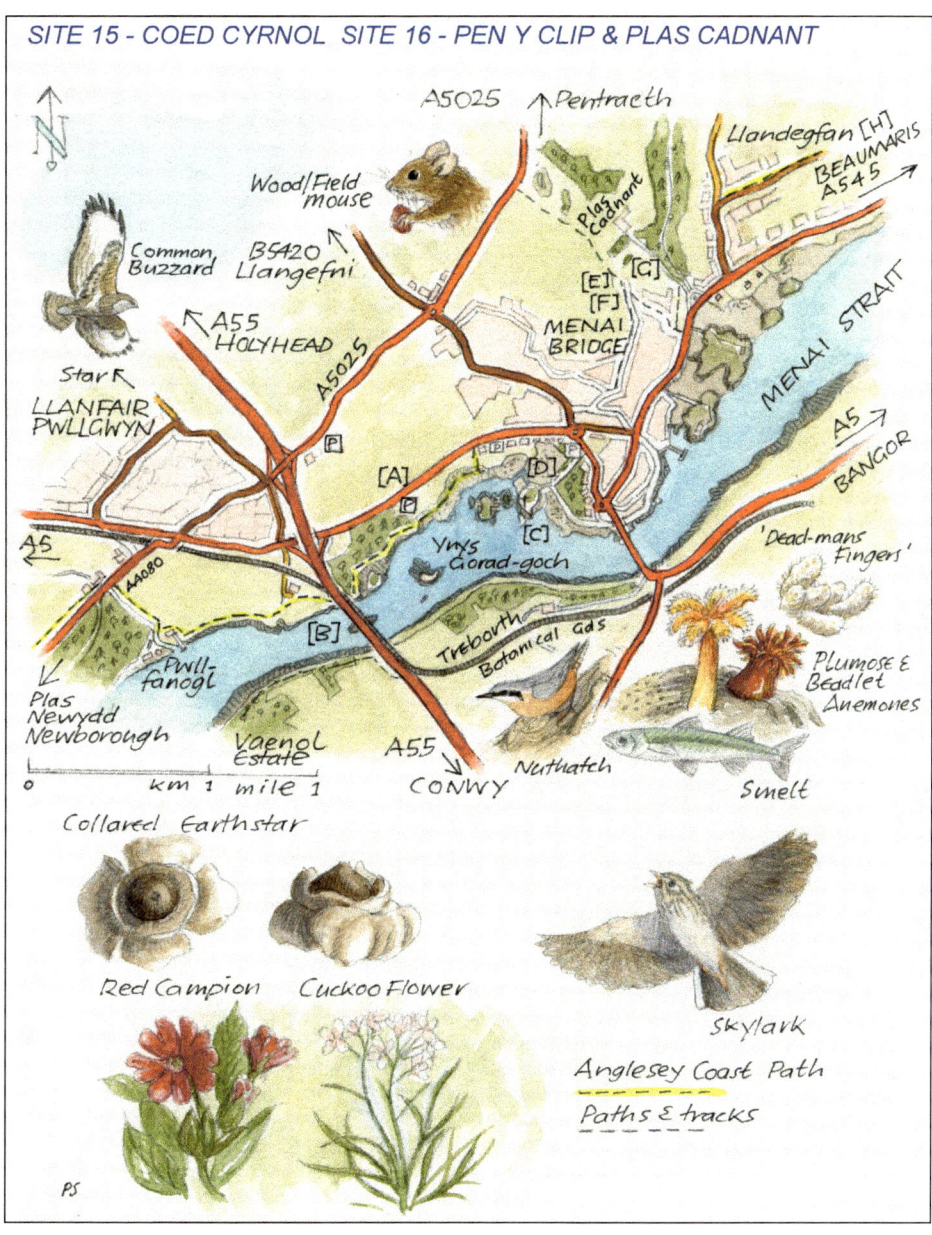

SITE 15 - COED CYRNOL SITE 16 - PEN Y CLIP & PLAS CADNANT

scan far and wide from its top. The trees are fairly open here and the understory generally drier than other local woods. Holly, yew, rowan and hazel are common among the usual oak, sycamore, ash and beech, but the woods are not particularly noted for either flowers, ferns, bryophytes or fungi. Red squirrels are increasingly seen, as all along the island's southern coastal woodland, road and gardens strip nowadays. The other popular attraction here is the fifteenth-century (at the very least) St Tysilio's Church and graveyard on its own little Church Island and

Blackcap.

causeway directly below the woods. The prom eventually leads around to the busy little town and quayside with its many boating activities, Marine Science Laboratory, busy restaurants and pubs.

Typical woodland and garden birds in the woods include common raven, wood pigeon, collared dove, great spotted woodpecker, nuthatch, treecreeper, carrion crow, jay, magpie, goldcrest, coal, long-tailed and other tits, and summer visitors like blackcap, chiff-chaff, willow and garden warbler, and, if you are fortunate, the now elusive spotted flycatcher. Among the rather more predictable robin, dunnock, wren, starling and thrushes, etc., families of partial albino, white-splashed blackbirds currently live around here despite the sparrowhawks that dwell in almost any setting nowadays, especially urban, or the peregrine falcons that have nested on Britannia Bridge. The bodacious falcons once surprised Treborth's Nigel Brown by dropping a fresh woodcock at his feet during their breathtaking 'sky dancing' display. Common buzzard, kestrel and tawny owl are the other common raptors, again showing the wealth of prey.

As for the Strait's great water life, we even see kingfishers fishing rock pools for common prawns, as by Church Island. Talking of master fishers, Ynys Gorad Gôch has a conspicuous (especially noticeable when the high tides are racing close to the house) fish weir, famous for providing 'whitebait teas' to Victorian and Edwardian folk. They were especially ferried over the dangerous waters in a little rowboat, by the enterprising owners. 'Whitebait' are the tiny young of many fish species, but mainly herring, mackerel and smelt hereabouts, cooked very quickly and eaten whole. We sometimes see large shoals of them literally driven ashore, leaving glittering, silvery swathes on the tideline, chased by adult mackerel, Atlantic bass and the like – their own parents! Yet then they in the turn are often chased by cetaceans and seals, also seen here on occasion. Much of the other typical marine life hereabouts, particularly the rich encrusting F&F, are covered in the preceding Site 14.

Then we have, to a lesser extent, the mammals. Otters are increasingly seen nowadays, plus many of the usual candidates, such as the three common bats (including noctule), red foxes – especially since the Britannia Bridge caught fire and was briefly closed in 1970 – and, probably, badgers. Less welcome, American mink and domestic ferrets are also observed around this area, the often creamy ferrets breeding with polecats (from whence they were originally bred for rabbiting), another mammal that has recently increased in north-west Wales. Nowadays, the biggest problem bridge-hopping mammal is that notorious 'alien invader', the grey squirrel, ever liable to recolonise Môn after being eradicated as the native red squirrel was successfully reintroduced (greys still need to be trapped along this section of coast to prevent that, as, ironically, the grey's deadly squirrel pox disease kills only reds, not the greys themselves). Other mammals like rabbit, brown hare, stoat, weasel, polecat, hedgehog, mole, and many of the usual voles, mice and shrew species can all be found around here somewhere, including dainty little yellow-necked wood mice, especially found in Treborth Gardens. Common frog and toad, too, with palmate newt, at least, and the usual reptiles like slow-worm and common lizard.

The other mixed, damper woodlands either side of the Strait are generally richer in plant life and fungi. Some fine ferns and over 100 bryophytes, including lots of liverworts and bark-encrusting lichens, are present in Treborth, or to a lesser degree by the Menai Bridge lay-by. Treborth is especially famed for its yearly Fungi Forays – as in September and October 2019 when some 210 species were found, including amazing earthstars and the cute little bird's-nest fungus.

As for insects, there's plenty of course, including six species of bumblebee and some twenty-nine of butterflies, including the uncommon and spectacular purple hairstreak (which is unfortunately largely found only high in the oaks), bright-yellow brimstone and subtle white-letter hairstreak. Note that there is also a brimstone moth, also bright yellow but smaller and with little brown markings, amid some 500 other moth species trapped at Treborth. They include several large, spectacular hawk moths, like lime and elephant hawk moths, although the large yellow underwing, silver Y and heart and dart are some of the commonest moths, as elsewhere around here.

The Coast Path now has to leave the coast entirely until virtually in Beaumaris (Site 18), but don't miss the lovely little gardens, stream, estuary and house of Plas Cadnant (Site 16), oftimes open to the public, or the next woodland and meadow site, just above Menai Bridge.

LNR, UCNW, RSTW, NRW, ACP

SITE 16: CAEAU PEN Y CLIP RESERVE AND THE CADNANT VALLEY
OS reference SH 558-728, 561-729.

Caeau Pen y Clip (E), the modest NWWT reserve on the outskirts of Menai Bridge, is, ironically, a sad reminder of what used to be considered 'normal' countryside in most of Britain – wildlife-rich meadows, field margins, boggy 'bottoms' and verdant hedgerows. Cuckoos and lapwings would have been calling, skylarks and yellowhammers singing, grey partridge 'chucking', and maybe a little tractor or even horse would be ploughing nearby, followed by skeins of gulls. Modern, post-war methods of farming have seen too much of that disappear, with the need for bigger fields and yields leading to the loss of hedgerows, verges and field

Red Squirrels—mating chase?
(note different colour 'phases'

Otter studies, from both wild
& captive creatures

Above: Red squirrels, play or mating. *Below:* Otter studies, from wild and captivity.

headlands. At least many are now aware of the problem and trying to redress it, given the huge environmental, sociological and economic implications.

Meanwhile, these old-fashioned reminders here on Anglesey make for a pleasant little stroll and is a chance to experience this 'haven for wildlife', as the trust describes it. Unfortunately, there is little or no parking on the two roads that abut both ends of the public footpath that passes through it, one on the main Pentraeth road and the other at the official entrance at the top of Menai Bridge's little Druid Road (F).

This entry sets the tone, though, with its green tunnel of trees and rich hedgerows, eventually opening out into the five fields that make up the reserve. The largest field is dominated by an area of marshy grassland, a typically good place to see wintering common snipe, and where the likes of corncrake, lapwing and redshank often nested until comparatively recently. Many flowering and other plants abounded, and small mammals like harvest mouse might at least still hang on.

The mature hedgerows and small trees can host a variety of breeding birds from usual garden birds like robin, dunnock, wren, blackbird, song and mistle thrush, pied wagtail, several tits and bright finch species – including linnet, chaffinch, goldfinch and bullfinch – to summer visitors like whitethroat, blackcap, willow warbler and chiff-chaff – and, if you are fortunate, lesser whitethroat or one of our few cuckoos. The nearby mature gardens and woods of Plas Cadnant, partially in view from the fields, mean there will be many other birds around, like wood pigeons, several of the crow family (including common raven and rook), and winter flocks of starling, fieldfare and redwing.

The mammals include several vole species (short-tailed field vole, for sure), mice like the common wood/field mouse and possibly all three shrews, including the water shrew. As for bats, they are certainly common enough at dusk and include the usual two pipistrelles, brown long-eared, and possibly noctule – and others. This cannot be a definite list, and environmental organisations are delighted to receive your records of any F&F, especially with detailed descriptions and photos or sketches. Likewise with reptiles and amphibians, which are also not well recorded – or at least published – from here or many other places on Anglesey. This is your chance to add to our knowledge.

Naturally, this is mainly a reserve of plants, flowers and insects. Later in the year, the hedges and trees provide a good selection of nuts, berries and haws for autumn and winter wildlife. Typical Anglesey wetland and damp meadow wildflowers here include cuckoo flower, purple loosestrife, ragged robin and yellow rattle, water mint, early purple and common spotted orchid, butterbur, marsh cinquefoil, yellow flag iris and juncus and other rushes.

Dabchick // Little Grebe.
Summer & winter

Little grebe.

Just to the east of the main path, the beautiful Plas Cadnant gardens (G) can be seen and are well worth a visit in themselves. Its old house, walled garden, wooded canyon-like stream and falls – and red squirrels – as well as café, holiday cottages and apartments, make it a national garden 'treasure' and regularly open to the summer public. Down below, the eastern edge of Menai Bridge has several good viewpoints out onto rocky little bays and private islets, often rich with seasonal wildfowl and waders, or the grey heron and little egret, that nest on some of them. Shelduck and mute swan usually also breed on their edges or shallow bays. And where the little Afon Cadnant enters the Strait, the old road wiggles down to a picturesque old stone bridge, which offers great views both upstream to the old mill house or out onto a little estuary and several islets. Kingfisher and little grebe usually winter here, among the aforementioned waterbirds, including the omnipresent mallard. Not that you can see much of that from the soulless new bridge of the A545 that bypasses it. Note that the road also serves as the Coast Path here, and eastwards from Menai Bridge, before turning up the steep hill to Llandegfan. Henceforth, it parallels the largely inaccessible coast on the lower (H) and quieter of the two roads through Llandegfan that eventually lead over to Beaumaris.

NWWT, LNR, ACP, Plas Cadnant

SITE 17: CYTTIR MAWR RESERVE, LLANDEGFAN
OS reference SH 577-750

This intimate little LNR woodland (A) is split by the top road from Llandegfan to Beaumaris, and adjacent to the Llan y Gors Fishing Lakes and campsite (B). It is a rather damp wood dominated by birch and willow, with a good scattering of young oak, damson and sloe, and threaded by tracks and duck boards. It's also testament to how quickly some trees grow, with traces of the heathland it was not so long ago still showing on modern maps, and in the few grassy or mossy glades, heathers and gorses, ferns, blackberry, and little limestone outcrops. Just one nightjar-looking piece of open heathland is left nowadays after a severe fire, and to quote the LNR website: 'Cyttir Mawr demonstrates the process of habitat succession: heathland that has reverted to woodland as a result of the discontinuation of grazing. There is evidence of some small-scale quarrying at the reserve'.

It also has a few small ponds – some which appear seasonal, or possibly limestone 'sink wells'? – hence the presence of uncommon water-beetles, and probably newts, as well as typical rushes and flowering broad-leaved pondweed. It can also boast two rather esoteric-sounding fungi among the sixty-five species recorded. These are the 'hairy bonnet' and the 'snake-tongue truffleclub'. Note the 'truffleclub' was previously unknown on the island – possibly because it is not only small, dark and unobtrusive but doesn't look like a snake-tongue, and that the 'hairy bonnet' is not even in most fungi books. Ferns are also well represented here, if, as per usual, dominated by the large royal fern and distinctive, un-branched hart's tongue.

As well as the now almost ubiquitous red squirrel on Anglesey, other mammals include mole, and I have little doubt, red fox, hedgehog, wood mouse and various shrews and bat species, as commonly seen in the neighbourhood. The birds around

SITE 17 - CYTTIR MAWR   SITE 18 - MENAI STRAIT TO BEAUMARIS

here are also typical, dominated by families of noisy jays, jackdaws, common ravens and wood pigeons, with great spotted woodpecker and familiar woodland-garden birds like robin, dunnock, and various tits, finches and thrushes (including redwing and fieldfare in winter), and summer warblers like blackcap, willow and chiff-chaff. Green woodpeckers used to be common around here, even more so than the rest of the island. Typical hedgerow and woodland flowers include the

Green woodpecker.

red campion, with associated butterflies and moths like the speckled wood, or winter moth, although its female is flightless.

Now, this part of south-east Anglesey is rather different to the more open western and northern parts of the island, with its little fields, streams, hedgerows and small stands and copses of woodland, which has some magnificent old oaks. Large gardens, too, hence the presence of red squirrels and typical woodland garden birds, and a whole network of paths and little lanes. Note that the footpath southwards through Cyttir Mawr now goes through the extensive series of fishing pools recently established by Llyn y Gors 'Coarse Fishing & Holiday Complex' – and that they ask any walkers to respect that, by keeping to the path. However, that also means that kingfishers are now seen here, as are otters, and from a much improved footpath – until you re-enter the typically boggy fields of the area that is. That's also often the case once you leave the delightful little lane alongside the eastern side of the reserve, or the lower Llandegfan road it joins, and venture onto other footpaths, especially in winter. The one behind the reservoir at Pen-y-Parc (C) is particularly marshy and undulating, before the Coast Path joins the steep lane downhill into Beaumaris. The Welsh Water lake itself is well worth a viewing from further back up the lane for its damp woodlands, great crested grebe, tufted duck, white water lilies and pink water bistort, but please note 'No Unauthorised Entry'. That also applies to the strip of private woodland to the south of the path and lake, but it is one of the few places you could find the elusive lesser spotted woodpecker on Anglesey and, until recently, golden pheasant – both were seen from the path. Unfortunately, there is little parking on the narrow lanes round here, bar a little lay-by around half a mile away by Llandegfan.

LNR, ACP

SITE 18: MENAI STRAIT SHORELINE, GALLOWS POINT, BEAUMARIS TO PENRHYN POINT
OS reference SH 577-750, 630-795

This is where the Strait really opens out and all manner of sea and shore birds are possible, dependent on tide and season. The rest of the shoreline back to Menai

Top: Wigeon pair

Right : Teal pair

Bottom : Oystercatchers

Above: Wigeon pair. *Middle:* Teal pair. *Below:* Adult oystercatchers in summer and winter.

Bridge is dominated by an extensive strip of largely inaccessible mixed private woodland bordering both the Strait and the twisting corniche main road, which is now great for red squirrel. The only viewpoints in this stretch are the Gazelle pub's handy veranda (E), or Plas Rhianfa's terraced gardens. Both are more or less opposite Bangor Pier, which recently (2019) hosted a rare common seal, and red-necked grebe among the usual Strait waterbirds like red-breasted merganser, goldeneye, great crested grebe, and the usual gulls, including winter common gull.

Gallows Point (D) is the next good viewpoint, with plentiful shore access around the garage, boatyard and chandlery. The little headland is ideally placed opposite the main mussel-farming beds, which are probably responsible for attracting breeding eider ducks in recent years, although they've wintered around Wales for some time and are still generally heading southwards in Britain. The other attraction is large high-tide roosts of waders like oystercatchers, curlew, redshank, dunlin, ringed plover and knot, especially in winter.

The large yacht-filled bay between here and Beaumaris can also hold a lot of those commoner waders, plus shelduck, wigeon and even brent geese nowadays, the latter two in non-breeding times, with the usual grey heron and little egret. There is an attractive little beech woodland just behind the shore at (F), which has hosted wood warbler and redstart in the past, so always worth a look.

From Beaumaris onwards, the wide shore varies from boulders, shingle, sand and mud, so beloved of many birds as well as human bait diggers. In fact the overharvesting of rag and king ragworm here has become a problem, although the wet, rocky stretches hold a host of other shore life, including lugworm, or peacock and bootlace worms. Then there's the various crabs, anemones, common prawns and shrimps, or small fish like butterfish, clingfish and sand gobies. Although the seaweed is dominated by serrated wrack and oarweed, we also have small areas of the scarce dwarf eelgrass, plus the usual mass of shellfish like common cockles and mussels, carpet shells, razor clams, common winkle and periwinkle, dog whelks, and even introduced New Zealand oysters (ours have been more or less fished out). Hence the Strait is home to a wide variety of shore and wading birds, as well as those already mentioned. Others include whimbrel, ringed plover, turnstone, both godwits, greenshank, spotted redshank, common, curlew and purple sandpipers, and grey, green and golden plovers, if all in various habitats, numbers and seasons. Amongst the wealth of sea fowl often just offshore, we have increasing and internationally important flocks of common scoter.

In the summer, terns are one of the main attractions, including sandwich, common, Arctic and the odd roseate, little or black terns (even a rare American Forster's tern has briefly wintered), fishing or passing. Closer to Penmon at Trwyn Penrhyn, there can be plentiful auks, such as guillemot, razorbill, Atlantic puffin and, year-round, the increasing black guillemot. Many of these nest on Puffin Isle (Site 25), along with great cormorant and shag, or the plentiful gulls hereabouts including great and lesser black-back, herring, black-headed and common gulls. Fulmars, too, and maybe kittiwakes, both of which also nest on the isle. Nowadays, seemingly due to returning herring and mackerel, northern gannets are especially seen from early spring to late autumn around Môn, as can Manx shearwaters, especially when gales drive them further into the Strait (look out for the odd, rare sooty or Balearic shearwaters). Eider ducks and red-breasted merganser are now here year-round, although the various skuas and petrels, like the great, Arctic, pomarine and odd long-tailed skua, or storm and Leach's petrels, are mainly autumn visitors generally on their way south.

From autumn onwards, the Strait hereabouts – and by the mainland opposite – is home to an ever bigger variety of waterbirds, from those already mentioned to the odd velvet or even American surf scoter, long-tailed duck, scaup and goldeneye,

Long-tailed ducks.

as well as lots of great crested grebes and the odd black-necked, Slavonian or red-necked. Potentially, we also have all the Eurasian divers (counting the one rare white-billed diver record from Holyhead), but certainly several great northern, red-throated and the odd black-throated diver are regular here. A telescope is important though, as the birds can be quite distant.

Otter, grey seal, bottle-nosed dolphin and common (harbour) porpoise are all possible here, if sporadic, excepting the seals, especially the nearer one gets to Puffin Isle. The marine life and fish are generally as for Menai Bridge, especially flatfish like plaice and more oceanic species as the Strait filters out. Several of the bird species indicate plentiful shellfish, thus comparatively shallow waters, and up until around one hundred years ago, a causeway linking Puffin Isle and the mainland was visible at very low tides, and Beaumaris was still where the main route across the Strait terminated until the bridges were built (see Ashton's *The Battle of Land & Sea*).

ANOB, NT, ACP

SITE 19: HENLLYS WOODS AND LLYN BODGYLCHED, BY BEAUMARIS
OS reference SH 599-777, 588-770

The countryside behind Beaumaris, especially attractive with its high, undulating ridge of woodland and steep little valleys and lanes, small fields and copses, contain all manner of F&F typical of south-west Anglesey. Because of that and its openness to easterly winds, it is also the wettest and most likely part of the island to get snow. Yet it's wildlife is relatively unknown, barring the red squirrel woodland at Henllys Hall (A), by the golf course and luxury apartments of the same name at Llanfaes. Currently (2019) there are still weekly guided walks by RSTW (Red Squirrels Trust Wales), but please check beforehand, or for access generally as there are few public footpaths, if many little lanes, hereabouts. The birds are the usual woodland and field/garden species, like common buzzard, sparrowhawk,

SITE 19 - HENLLYS & BODGYLCHED. 20 - LLANGOED & ABERLLEINIOG
21 - MARIANDYRYS 22 - FEDW FAWR 23 - BWRDD ARTHUR 24 - LLANDDONA COMMONS

Fulmar Petrel &
Herring gull
adults

White Beach
&
Fedwr Fawr

Coed y
Hendy
[M]

P [J]

Small
P-bordered
Fritillary

Mariandyrys

[H]

Penmon

[I]

Bwrdd
Arthur

Gorse

Frog
Orchid
[G]

Red Wharf Bay

Llangoed
[C]

Llanlog
[E]

[D]

Kestrel ♀

[F]

B5109

BEAUMARIS

[L]
Llaniestyn
Common

Llanddona

[K]
Llanddona
Common

Henllys [A]

Werny
Wylah

ps

Llyn
Bodgylched
[B]

Weasel & Rabbit

0   km 1   mile 1

B5109

Anglesey Coast Path

Pentraeth
Paths & tracks

BEAUMARIS

Sparrowhawk.

jay, green, great spotted and sometimes lesser-spotted woodpeckers, nuthatch, treecreeper, goldcrest, wood pigeon and stock dove, robin, wren, dunnock, the usual tits, finches, thrushes, wagtails, typical warblers like chiff-chaff and willow warbler in summer, and a few otherwise declining spotted flycatchers.

The rather mixed and sometimes straggly woods of ash, hazel, elder, beech, oak, Scots pine and holly, etc., certainly have masses of flowers like wild garlic, bluebell, lesser celandine, assorted ferns like hart's tongue, typical bryophytes like lichens and mosses, and mammals like red fox and plentiful smaller rodents, as well as red squirrels. As this is not a particularly well watched area, all records are welcome. Atop the ridge, by the Llandonna road, there is a hidden gem of a wetland called Llyn Bodgylched (B), partially viewable from the footpath that also passes the prominent Bulkeley Memorial. Unfortunately there is little parking here. The lake has the usual wildfowl of the island, wetland warblers like sedge, plus reed bunting and hirundines like swallow, house and sand martin, and can be a bit of a draw for the declining swift in late spring. Hen harrier, bittern, nightjar, hobby and crane have all been seen, although largely uncommon of course, but marsh harriers are another typical returnee to such wetlands in the not-so-distant past.

Henllys Hall, RSTW

SITE 20: LLANGOED COMMON AND ABERLLEINIOG
OS reference SH 610-797

The quiet little village of Llangoed (C) has several good, radiating wildlife walks, largely centred on the two rushing little rivers that dissect it. They join up in the damp woods at (D) before entering the Strait at Lleiniog (E). In the woods, roughly halfway down to the Strait, is Aberlleiniog Local Nature Reserve, which contains the remains of a motte-and-bailey castle, now a Scheduled Ancient Monument. It was built (or rebuilt on an older site?) by the invading Normans in the eleventh

Above left: Common blue damselfly. *Above right:* Stonechat. *Middle left:* Cuckoo flower and orange tip. *Middle right:* Slender parasol. Bottom: Lapwings and golden plover.

Water shrew.

century and refortified during the English Civil War, although the present structure seems to have be rebuilt as a folly, probably in the nineteenth century.

To paraphrase the official blurb, the F&F of the area is 'wonderfully diverse', from lots of birds (especially songbirds including redpoll and siskin, or raptors like sparrowhawk and tawny owl), to mammals like red squirrel, otter, several bat species and water shrew, with amphibians like common frog and toad, several newt species, reptiles like common lizard, slow-worm and adder, and lots of invertebrates like butterflies, dragonflies and damselflies. All in, 'ancient woodland flora, mature and young wet broadleaf woodland, wet and wild-flower meadows, open glades and rides, hedgerows, ponds and the Afon Lleiniog'. Like many little Anglesey rivers nowadays, there will often be kingfisher, grey wagtail and dipper somewhere along their lengths.

Starting by the bridge in the village, a concrete road initially heads Strait-wards, eventually joining a wonderful, meandering boardwalk through damp, flower-rich woods and up to the castle. Marsh marigold is a typical early spring flower, plus bluebell, lesser celandine and early purple orchid, with the usual ferns, lichens and mosses sometimes draping the trees. The rest of the tracks can be rather muddy, especially (F), which (2019) is still very narrow, wet, undulating and unfortunately subject to rubbish dumping, despite being an AONB.

Llangoed Common is a narrow little LNR (G) that has the typical wet pasture flowers like meadow and other buttercups, may or cuckooflower, ragged robin, and the subtle little marsh cinquefoil. It is bordered by the stream and a footpath paralleling the little road up to Glan-yr-Afon, and Mariandwrys Nature Reserve (Site 21). Also of note nearby is Cornelyn Manor, now private dwellings but formerly the home of the celebrated Massey sisters, whose superb nineteenth-century paintings of virtually all of Môn's wildflowers now grace the walls and books of Oriel Môn.

At the other end, the wooded footpath by the damp, Snipey meadows and winding river – with its small brown trout and other fish – opens up to fine views of the Menai Strait, from the Great Orme to the Carneddau and Snowdonia mountain ranges. There is a largish parking area and picnic site here, right by the naturally subsiding, Ice Age, boulder-clay cliffs and little river estuary, and wide views of the Strait and all its varied wildlife, especially shore and seabirds, as per Site 18.

LNR, NWWT, AONB, SAM, Rural Development Agency, Menter Môn

SITE 21: MARIANDYRYS COMMON

SITE 22: FEDW FAWR

SITE 23: BWRDD ARTHUR

SITE 24: LLANDONNA COMMON
OS *references: SH 809-605, SH 605-818, SH 587-813, SH 576-796*

Mariandyrys Common (H) is a fine, prominent reserve with flower-rich grassland, heath and gorse, on dry rocky outcrops, grykes, layered cliffs and quarries. These are all typical of limestone, and locally common in North Wales, from Llangollen to the Great Orme and Anglesey. Known largely for its interesting plants, this NWWT Reserve (and others nearby) has many representative flowers including common rock rose, blue spring squill, yellow tormentil, wild thyme, trefoils, violets, heathers and several species of fern like the common hart's tongue. Lime-loving orchids too, like the early purple, bee, pyramid, and possibly fragrant and lesser butterfly orchids – do watch where you tread! It is also naturally a great habitat for insects, especially moths and butterflies. Over twenty species of the latter have been recorded including small pearl-bordered fritillary, grayling and the rare brown argus. As for other insects and allies, as usual there are far too many to mention here, but look out for industrious colonies of yellow meadow ants, or many ladybirds, spiders, bees, hoverflies, shield bugs, and especially bright beetles like the tiger beetle and iridescent rose chafer. Glow-worms are possible here, as in the drier, north-east parts of Môn generally.

Stonechat, meadow pipit, linnet and whitethroat are the typical, most prominent birds of open scrub and heathland, although you might only spot some of the larger insects like emperor moths in a stonechat's bill. Note also that the declining yellowhammer used to be fairly common hereabouts and on the whole east coast of Anglesey, as did cuckoo, but both are still possible, especially at Cors Gôch (Site 28). Heaths are still good places for reptiles like adder, common lizard and slow-worm, all of which can be found basking in the sun if you are quiet. Small mammals like wood/field mice or short-tailed voles and various shrews account for the hovering kestrel or common buzzard's attentions, while rabbits can attract an evening red fox, stoat, weasel or polecat. Brown hares, thankfully, are still here and widespread on Anglesey.

The elevated reserve also supplies great all-round views of the local windmill and Puffin Isle, Great Orme, Carneddau and Snowdonia, or even the Isle of Man, Lake District and Blackpool Tower on a clear day, plus lots of cargo vessels and wind turbines. Unfortunately, parking is restricted so please be careful where you leave cars – field and farm gates are often in use, verges good for flowers.

A little further north and closer to the cliffs, the not dissimilar Bwrdd Arthur ('Arthur's Table'), or Din Silwy Iron Age hill fort (I), is a prominent if small limestone hill overlooking the dramatic cliffs, slopes and forest decorating the margins of Red Wharf Bay. Its typical, flat-topped limestone terrain is noted for its extensive pre-Roman to Viking history, as well as being an SSSI, designated

Top : Pipistrelle Bat

Right : Wood/Field Mouse

Bottom : Brown Hare

Above left: Pipistrelle bat. *Above right:* Wood/Field mouse. *Below:* Brown hare.

Red fox.

for botanical riches. These include much as the preceding site, plus the rare hoary rockrose alongside early purple and (uncommon, exotic) frog orchids, with aromatic marjoram, bright greater knapweed and glorious blue cornflowers on the summer road verges below.

Once again, the birds will be dominated by meadow pipit and stonechat, but with spiralling skylark, kestrel, peregrine and corvids like jackdaw and common raven working the whirling winds above. There are reptiles and insects too. The tiny medieval church of St Deiniol or St Michael is on the eastern side, below the hill fort, with impressive old yews, but has limited parking. Also note some of the footpaths are quite steep and sometimes overgrown.

Fedw Fawr's (J) steep, cliff-girt coast used to be the only black guillemot site on Môn until their recent revival, which once again sees them around much of the island's coast, even nesting in Holyhead harbour. White Beach, with its bright, white cobbled shore and jade-green sea, is nearby, its ledges a popular fishing spot, as well as great for looking down on fishing black guillys (note they are largely white in winter) wrestling with butterfish in the clear waters. Along with other regular coast and breeding birds, fulmar petrels, though declining in line with our fishing industry, should still be patrolling these cliffs. Grey seals are another delight when seen underwater in such clear seas, their creamy cubs another big draw in the autumn.

Further south-west, Llandonna Common (K) is yet another rich limestone coastal flowering heath that has similar birds, flowers, small mammals, reptiles, butterflies and insects. The whole area is basically a patchwork of small fields, flower-rich grassland and dry heathland either side of Llandonna village. The nearby Rhos Llaniestyn Common (L) is a similar pony-grazed habitat of dry scrub, heathland and marshy grassland – so winter snipe and common frog and toad are probable. Note the attractive little lane down to Wern y Wylan, Pentraeth Forest and Red Wharf Bay, which has lots of hazel in its lower hedges, and hence good for the red squirrels (Site 26), whose last stronghold this was before their general reintroduction.

NWWT, ACP, LNR

SITE 25: PUFFIN ISLAND AND PENMON
OS reference SH 640-812

Now here's an island for names and history. Although named Ynys Seriol in favour of the Christian saint who inhabited it in the fifth and sixth centuries, it was also called Ynys Lannog or Glannauc. That is until the Vikings (namers of 'Angles-Eye') renamed it Priestholm. Puffin Isle (A) is a comparatively recent designation, naturally named for the charismatic bird, although another invasion in the late twentieth century, by brown rats, almost saw them off, until their removal allowed the hole-nesting puffin, and many other ground-nesting seabirds, to return. If the rats weren't bad enough, St Seriol apparently used to pickle the puffins, exporting them as far away as Europe. Well, he also founded Penmon Monastery (B), which has a typical dovecot and holy well, before setting up the community on the island. The Point (opposite) is now graced with a coastguard lookout and cottages, café, and trademark black and white lighthouse. There is also a small wooded pool by the well and tollbooth (there is a charge to drive over to Penmon Point), where firecrests often winter among the regular garden/woodland birds. Note also a little wooded valley footpath at (M), Coed y Hendy, where yellow-browed warbler, another typical if skulking autumn migrant, is sometimes seen.

Just before the priory, a small pool in the field to the left (C) often has lots of typical sea and shore birds on or around its shallow margins, like the omnipresent resident geese or gulls, and is also one of the likeliest places on Môn to see yellow wagtail in the spring (note similarity to resident grey wagtails).

As we approach the rougher seas around Penmon and the island, the rocks are dominated by a tougher mixture of seaweeds, with common mussels, periwinkle and acorn barnacle species common among them, and many crustaceans, etc. With several large limestone quarries locally, red valerian, and even bee and other orchids, naturally abound, as well as smaller birds like rock and meadow pipits, stonechat, or corvids and peregrine. (Note though that the quarry is dangerous and off-limits.) Hummingbird hawkmoths are likely to be seen on any such flower-rich slopes in summer, as well as the usual butterflies like common blue and gatekeeper. Nowadays the attractive, silvery limestone Ynys Seriol, or Puffin Isle, is privately owned, and both a SSSI and SPA (Special Protection Area), so the best way to see it is by one of the many boat or fishing trips out from Beaumaris. Along with its twelfth-century church and modern telegraph station remains, it also boasts one of the largest, if very stunted, elder woods in the UK. This stretches along much of the lee or south-eastern slopes, and is thought to be one result of the decline in rabbits due to myxomatosis – the lack of nesting holes for puffins is another. Its typically layered Carboniferous limestone cliffs, bays and slopes host lots of birds, besides the puffins, although most now nest out on the Skerries (Site 48). Shags nest down near the waters edge, then the untidy nests of kittiwakes, while fulmars and jostling lines of guillemots and razorbills typically utilise the higher, flatter ledges. Feral/cross rock doves nest too, plus the usual gulls, minus black-headed, if mainly on the roughly vegetated slopes and rocks. Finally, a long ragged line of great cormorants breed about the rocky ridge of the island, with red-breasted merganser and eider duck nesting on lower vegetated slopes, as well as the usual rock pipits and stonechat.

SITE 25 - PUFFIN ISLAND & PENMON

Common Dolphin   Grey Seals

Red Valerian

[A] PUFFIN ISLE

Bee Orchid

Quarry

Penmon Point

Puffin

[M]

Penmon Priory

[B]

[D] Caim

Quarry

Lesser-spotted Catshark (Dogfish)

Llanddona

Penmon

[C]

Llangoed
Castell
Aberlleiniog

MENAI STRAIT

BEAUMARIS B5109

Lleiniog

Yellow & Grey Wagtails

0   km 1   mile 1

Anglesey Coast Path   Paths & tracks

Seabelt or Sugarkelp; top: Oarweed or Tangle

Puffin Isle and Penmon Point.

Grey seals regularly fish and pup on the lowest rocks and bays, while bottle-nosed and common dolphins and harbour porpoises frolic and fish, or breed in the porpoises case, around much of this rocky coast. Please note that puffins usually leave their UK nest sites for the open sea by early August.

Heading back from Penmon Point, the joint Wales/Anglesey Coast Path heads inland through Caim deer park (D), although you will search in vain for them nowadays. What you can see here are some of the many fossils, mainly marine shells and coral remains, in the massive, water-deposited Carboniferous limestone rocks that span some 170 degrees of the earth's surface.

SSSI, SPA, Geo-Môn. ACP, Gwynedd Archaeological Trust

SITE 26: RED WHARF BAY

SITE 27: PENTRAETH FOREST
OS reference SH 535-799

This huge sandy bay was clearly carved by much more than its present little river, which enters by the equally sandy beach car park (A) down a lane from Pentraeth, before meandering seawards (beware driving on the car park's soft margins!). The Coast Path also more or less follows the river, sometimes muddily along the western side, before reaching the much sandier northern shores. This part of the bay is frequently bounded by the usual limestone cliffs and damp woods of the area, then the busy little enclave of Red Wharf Bay, which has parking, pubs, camping, beaching and boating activities (B) (the opposite side of the bay is mainly

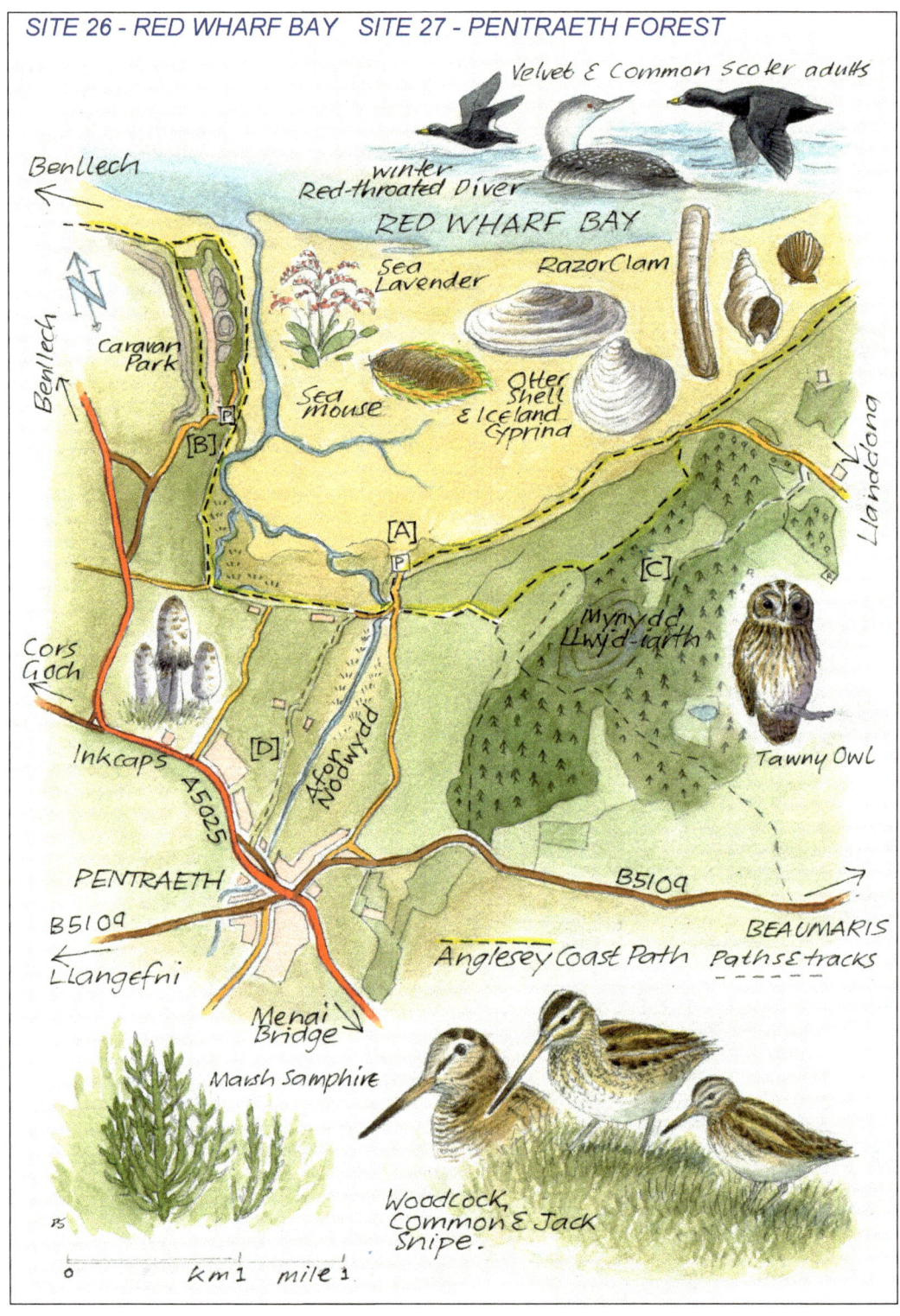

SITE 26 - RED WHARF BAY   SITE 27 - PENTRAETH FOREST

Velvet & Common Scoter adults

winter
Red-throated Diver

RED WHARF BAY

Benllech

Benllech

Caravan
Park

[B]

P

Sea
Lavender

RazorClam

Sea
mouse

Otter
Shell
& Iceland
Cyprina

Llanddona

[A]

P

[C]

Cors
Goch

Mynydd
Llwyd-iarth

Inkcaps

A5025

[D]

Afon Nodwydd

Tawny Owl

PENTRAETH

B5109

Llangefni

B5109

BEAUMARIS

Anglesey Coast Path   Paths & tracks

Menai
Bridge

Marsh Samphire

Woodcock,
Common & Jack
Snipe.

0   km 1   mile 1

Mallard and shelduck.

accessed by a rather steep, frequently single-track lane down from Llandonna). Note also that the Coast Path also straggles down from Bwrdd Arthur before skirting the entire bay's frequently flooded and lumpy margins – good boots or wellies are advised. Some of these edges are saltmarsh, especially below the forest, and seasonal host to a whole slew of birds from waders including redshank and common snipe (plus the odd jack snipe) to water rail, reed bunting, grasshopper warbler, cuckoo and barn owl. Note what look like human cockleshell 'middens', possibly hundreds of years old, being exposed in the eroding saltmarsh by the rusty wreck. The usual year-round cliff birds abound, too, especially on the steep eastern point and old quarries, with attendant rock pools, as on the opposite shore round to Benllech. There can be masses of birds out on the sands at low water, which incidentally also require caution, as fast incoming tides and a whole morphing maze of sand bars and gullies are not always apparent.

Shelduck are still common enough here, especially in winter, as are large flocks of waders like oystercatcher, green and golden plover (or the odd grey), redshank, dunlin, ringed plover, knot and curlew. There's always the possibility of whimbrel, turnstone, both godwits, greenshank, spotted redshank, or common, curlew and purple sandpipers, as well as the odd green or even wood sandpiper dropping in too. Grey herons and little egrets naturally abound, while, just once, a superb little green heron carried all the way from the Caribbean by autumn gales. Just offshore there are often good flocks of sea fowl, especially in non-breeding times, like red-throated diver and great crested grebe, common scoter, wigeon, red-breasted merganser and, in the autumn especially, piratical skuas including the elegant long-tailed skua. They especially target the various terns, themselves stoking up for the long haul south, and, as elsewhere, the usual five gull species, northern gannet and Manx shearwater dominate the busy 'passing trade'.

Raptors also find this place irresistible, especially in non-breeding season, when peregrine, merlin, hen harrier and short-eared owl can all patrol its margins or wide sands. Sparrowhawk and common buzzard, too, even goshawk or red kite, and the forest once attracted a scarce rough-legged buzzard for several winters. When the large common raven roost in Newborough started declining, it was partly because many again gathered here on the heights by Mynydd Llwydiarth

(C), their charismatic calls echoing far and wide in the winter dusk. As with any conifers, red crossbills are always possible, as well as the usual range of woodland birds like tawny owl, wood pigeon, great spotted woodpecker, treecreeper, blackcap, chaffinch, siskin and coal tit, and winter woodcock. On the sloping tree copse and hedge-lined fields below mistle thrush and corvids dominate, although tree pipits have bred here, and there is a particularly attractive group of ice-green-backed, ring-necked pheasants around at the moment (2019).

Although there is only one river, the Afon Nodwydd, entering the bay by the sandy car park and scenic, humpy bridge, there are several other little streams. Their fish include the (indecisive!) nine- or ten-spined stickleback and grey mullet going at least some way up the Nodwydd, along with silver eel, sea trout and attendant otter and kingfisher.

Surrounding saltmarsh is more or less as at Malltraeth Bay (Site 10), which has some fifteen species on the Môn coast prefixed by 'sea', such as sea lavender, sea beet and sea aster, or marsh samphire, all here among the tough marsh grasses and marram. Marine life, too, is similar, as shown by the popularity of the bay for fishing, bait digging and gleaning, for lug and rag worms, common cockle, razor clam or lesser sand eel. Wonderful oddities like the fluorescent-bordered sea mouse occasionally wash up after storms, as well as masses of shells, assorted starfish and crab shells, catshark and whelk egg cases, or even predatory Caribbean snails. Most fish here are the usual Anglesey species, though, with the much-prized Atlantic bass often speeding through the clear autumn waves alongside diving goldeneyes – a great sight. Flatties such as plaice, dab and flounder are also common, as well as the omnipresent little sand goby, common shrimp and, unfortunately on this more sheltered east coast, occasional hordes of summer jellies like the stinging, red-brown lion's mane jellyfish.

Back to other highlights of the area, red squirrels once again call Pentraeth Forest a stronghold, which has many tracks, clearings and fine views out over Red Wharf Bay. On the north-west end of the bay, the boulders, cliffs and old quarry hold masses of the usual marine Carboniferous limestone fossils, especially lots of corals, often seen end on and sometimes resembling huge blocks of spaghetti. There is also a fine, sheltered footpath (D) down from the village, overlooking the little river valley and marsh, with typical woodland/hedge birds like jay and lesser whitethroat, mammals like otter and red fox, insects and flowers and fungi including the remarkable ink cap mushroom.

National Nature Reserve, Geo-Mon, ACP

SITE 28: CORS GOCH
OS reference SH 504-816

Cors ('bog, swamp') Gôch (A) is a particularly famed NWWT reserve, basically a sinuous limestone fen set in an end Ice Age vale, with picturesque rocky outcrops, all rich in birds, reptiles, amphibians, insects, wetland plants and flowers. It is both a SSSI and NNR, and 'an internationally important site and one of Wales's richest and most diverse nature reserves'. There is certainly a whole mosaic of attractive habitats and tracks, and because of underlying geology and hydrology,

SITE 28 - CORS GOGH

Llanerchymedd

N

Moelfre

Brynteg

B5108

BENLLECH

A5025

Barn Owl

Adders Tongue

CORS GOCH

P

[A]

[B]

Yellow-hammer

Pentraeth

B5110

Lon Lydan

Gt'd Beetle

Llanbedrgoch

Llangefni

Pentraeth

3-spined Stickleback ♂

Fen Pondweed

Marsh Fritillary

Chaffinch, Linnet & Redpoll males

Water Vole PS

0   km 1   mile 1

Paths & tracks

some are said to be 'unique'. A lot of this hinges on the subtle differences between fen and marsh, as over at Cors Ddyga (Site 13), and largely down to the shallow, lime-rich springs that feed Cors Gôch's reed beds and pools. This is also the case at nearby Cors Erddreiniog and Cors Bodeilio (Sites 29 and 33).

The clear waters of these wetland fens are home to its most important flora – some of these plants exist only in this type of highly alkaline habitat – including uncommon saw sedge, or great fen sedge and blunt-flowered sedge, lesser clubmoss, pretty bogbean, parasitic butterwort, aromatic bog myrtle, northern marsh orchid, marsh cinquefoil, marsh gentian and a whole range of waterweeds like fen pondweed and uncommon, rugged and hedgehog stoneworts. Yet acidic peat can also underlie these waters, and was probably dug here, resulting in some of the lakes –and even its name, 'Red Bog'? The wetland attracts many insects and allies, too, including the rare medicinal leech, and a great selection of dragonflies and damselflies (*Odonata*). The three Cors have recorded some seventeen species of dragonfly, including keeled skimmer, hairy dragonfly, black darter and southern damselfly among the commoner ones like common/red darter, broad-bodied chaser and common blue damselfly. Some of these fens have also hosted the nationally uncommon scarce blue-tailed damselfly, and locally scarce variable damselfly. All *Odonata* have fearsome nymphs inhabiting such shallow waters, along with other small fish and tadpole-gobbling creatures like the great-diving beetle, water boatman, and exotic water scorpions, as well as commoner water striders and whirligig beetles literally walking on water.

The nineteen species of butterfly include small copper, orange tip, common blue, small pearl-bordered fritillary and occasionally the rare and beautiful marsh fritillary butterfly. Many moths can be seen here too including the large emperor moth, although best seen in the evening, excepting the uncommon black and white day-flying argent and sable moth (compare with the common magpie moth) particularly associated with bog myrtle, so also seen on fens.

The south-eastern side of the reserve, both limestone and sandstone outcrops, slopes and grassland, supports another superb biotope: heathland. Various heathers and western gorse dominate, typically with mats of wild thyme, small flowers like common rockrose, pale-heath violet, tormentil, spring squill, and the scarce green-winged orchid, unique adder's tongue fern, and 'English' stonecrop on the

Magpie, argent and sable, six-spot burnet and cinnabar moths.

barer limestone. The various hedgerows, pastures and copses also support lots of commoner but no less welcome flowers. These drier areas also have lots of prominent insects like the various grasshoppers, crickets, beetles, spiders, ants, and many others, if not so noticeable. Stonechat, linnet, meadow pipit and skylark also like such areas.

Most birds here are the usual wetland types, including 'mere-hen', water rail, little grebe and tufted duck, grey heron, little egret, whitethroat, sedge and reed warblers, reed bunting, and summer hirundines, but with three specialities: breeding yellowhammer, cuckoo and barn owl. Bittern and marsh harrier are increasingly dropping in, as on most of our wetlands. Likewise the mammals are familiar, like water vole, water shrew and otter, or amphibians like common frog and toad, plus newts including great crested newt. Possibly the water-loving grass snake, too, although uncommon on Môn. Certainly, other reptiles like adder, common lizard and slow-worm are common enough, if elusive, the best place to see them being the rocky outcrops, especially in spring when warming up their 'cold' blood.

As for access, a path runs the length of the reserve, with boardwalks through the wetter parts and various other paths and tracks (B) including one with stepping stones over to another little road by a caravan park. The NWWT suggests various routes to suit, from short walks to day-long tours, or activities like pond dipping. The main access is at (A), on the B road just over a mile north of the little village of Llanbedrgoch, where there is a lay-by with limited parking and a nearby information board.

NWWT, NNR, SSSI

SITE 29: CORS ERDDREINIOG
OS reference SH 463-820

By far the largest of the three fens, this broad, breezy, open limestone reserve has fine views north over its waving reed beds to Mynydd Bodafon (B) (Site 30), and the fledgling Afon Lligwy. As with other nearby fens, Erddreiniog (A) has many key and sometimes unique wetland plants and flowers, along with attendant birds, mammals, amphibians, reptiles and insects. Hence it is an NNR, SSSI and SAC, as well as a RAMSAR site, for its international importance. Unfortunately, as with several Môn reserves, it only has limited roadside parking, mainly in the village of Capel Coch, including a small car park near the reserve entrance. Access is by foot only, down a narrow, often muddy track beside a cottage in the village. There is a hardcore track once down on the reserve (C), and boardwalk providing a fine circular route through some of the site. As the NRW blurb says, 'Sturdy shoes are recommended and the reserve is not accessible to wheelchairs or pushchairs.' You can also overlook some areas near the main road from Brynteg to Llanerchymedd, oftimes good places to see wintering hen and marsh harrier, short-eared owl, or merlin, peregrine, kestrel and local barn and little owls – and, nowadays, increasingly common red kite.

Nevertheless, it is the plant life that is of international import, in this rare type of wetland, the clear, lime water fen. As also the source of the Afon Cefni and reservoir where most of our drinking water originates, that's good news. The main habitat is the fen, but as often with the two other sites, there are also peat lands, floating vegetation, small lakes, pools, ditches, drier heath and woodland.

SITE 29 - CORS ERDDREINIOG   30 - MYNYDD BODAFON

Bllmm. Hen Hamer

A5025

Dulas
Amlwch

Little
Owl

[E]

[B]

MYNYDD
BODAFON

[F]

MOELFRE

Llanerchymedd

Maenaddwyn

Lesser
Butterfly
Orchid

Capel
Coch

[A]
CORS ERDDREINIOG

[D]
Llyn Yr Wyth-
Eidion

B5110 Brynteg

[C]

Common
Twayblade

LLANGEFNI

Spawn

Common Frog &
LLANGEFNI

PS

0   km   ½   mile   ½

- - - - - - Paths & tracks

Marsh gentian.

It all sits in former Ice Age lake basins that have gradually in-filled with clay, marl and peat sediments, with low wooded slopes and farmlands to east and west. Again, the wetland plants include many of those at Sites 28 and 33, if dominated here by acres of common reed, alongside the rare great fen sedge, black bog rush, blunt-flowered rush, and 'bulrush' (great reed mace). Flowering plants include yellow flag iris, the lovely bogbean, water bistort and water lily, plus parasitic bladderwort and the two rare stonewort waterweeds as at Cors Goch. The more open areas have bog myrtle, cotton grass, cross-leaved heath (a heather) and purple moor grass (*Molinia*). There are also spongy carpets of bright green sphagnum moss, a great natural conserver and storer of water, with fly-catching butterwort and round-leaved sundew also showing the poor, acidic nature of parts of this otherwise alkaline bog. Yet in such wetter, acid heath, the superb marsh gentian, with devil's-bit scabious and monk's hood, are also found, but as usual there are far too many plants to detail here, and all records are welcome.

Erddreiniog is also an internationally important orchid-rich habitat, with up to seven species seen at a time, in June, by some – including fly orchid, marsh fragrant orchid, marsh helleborine, northern and early marsh orchid and common twayblade, with lesser butterfly orchid and frog orchid also found nearby. Don't expect the frog orchid to look much like its namesake, unlike the fly orchid – and what of the rare 'Pugsley's marsh orchid' found here; just another spotted/marsh 'cross'?!

With all that wetland, dragonflies and damselflies abound, with twenty-one species recorded including common hawker, golden-ringed, emperor and hairy dragonflies, four-spotted chaser, keeled skimmer and the chic black darter. Among the many common, bright blue-favouring damselflies like the common blue, the rare and protected southern damselfly and scarce blue-tailed damselfly are sometimes found, or the locally scarce variable damselfly. The waters include lots of other water insects, like those already mentioned for Cors Gôch, but here include the uncommon Geyer's whorl snail amid many water snails, and possibly the large ramshorn snail, as in some Môn pools. Anglesey supposedly only has a few native fish species, like the three- and nine/ten-spined stickleback, rudd, brown/sea trout and silver eel, but others have been introduced for fishing. I suspect the three-spined stickleback, rudd and silver eel will be commonest here, certainly with little brown trout in the exiting river.

As for birds, sometimes a clear winter afternoon is best to see the many waders or waterbirds present here, often including whooper swan, or masses of 'murmurating' starlings, flocks of fieldfare and redwing or gathering pied wagtails, meadow pipits and assorted finches. Then there are those aforementioned raptors or the chance of a beautiful barn owl, slowly quartering the rustling reed beds, limned in pale gold by the setting sun. Such winter sunsets can also reflect off flocks of whooper swans flying in, and once lit up a solitary great grey shrike perched prominently atop a small tree – glorious!

Nowadays, such sights could easily contain a bittern, during any season, and also notorious reed bed lurkers such as water rails, sometimes only known by their raucous and unusual calls. Lapwings can breed as well as furnish the vale with large winter flocks, like the golden plover and curlew, and smaller groups of snipe. There's always the chance of the smaller jack snipe as well. Other typical wetland birds include grey heron and little egret, mallard, teal, gadwall, tufted duck and pochard, mute swan, 'mere-hen' and coot, great crested and little grebes, and kingfisher. We can't forget the increasing flocks of imported Canada and greylag geese, noisily clamouring and dominating many an Anglesey reserve or lake. The smaller birds include sedge and reed warblers, whitethroat and cuckoo in summer, as well as reed bunting, stonechat, linnet and, on the margins and wooded areas, the usual woodland/garden birds including many rooks and jackdaws. Unfortunately, a famous local rarity, willow tit, has not been seen here for years. Bright yellowhammers should still be around, although also declining. There is a bird hide at (D), by the end of the boardwalk, largely overlooking the little lake of Llyn yr Wyth Eidion, named for a colourful local legend about what it reputedly swallowed whole, as I will leave you to discover. There are also various little wildlife pools dug beside the boardwalk should you wish to pond dip, supervised or not – please always remember to handle and return everything carefully; a flat, white plastic tray or large pickle jar is ideal for studying the various scurrying creatures, from daphnia to various freshwater shrimps and beetles, larvae, fish and damselfly and dragonfly nymphs.

Brown hares are resident, along with other mammals like otter, red fox, polecat, stoat, weasel, rabbit, the usual species of mice, voles and shrews including water shrew, and regular Môn bat species like pipistrelles, brown long-eared and possibly the 'water bat' (Daubenton's). As with many reserves, ponies and cattle are needed to graze (and fertilise) the reserve and keep some of the ranker, engulfing plants down, even reeds and rushes, thus encouraging the many lovely flowers and plants such places rightly boast.

NNR, SAC, SSSI, RAMSAR, IPA (Important Plant Area)

SITE 30: MYNYDD BODAFON
OS reference SH 468-850

Bodafon Mountain, or Mynydd Bodafon (B), is a rather grandly named collection of small hills that nevertheless pack a pretty punch. Mainly rocky and heather clad, with a charming little lake, they do include the highest point on Anglesey, the fairly easily accessible Arwydd or 'Signal' (E), thus ensuring great all-round views. Thanks to springs through the pale Precambrian quartzite, the mountain has several other small water bodies including two covered reservoirs and a number of little streams, which have footpath access. The presence of several woods and forestry on the south-eastern side also ensures that red squirrels, as elsewhere on Môn, are present.

True to its breezy, open heights, the wildlife centres upon typical heath plant life, birds, reptiles and lots of different insects. Indeed, one of the hill's most enduring images is of the wonderful purple, yellow and green patchwork of summer plants amid silvery rocks. Heathers dominate, consisting of ling, cross-leaved heath and bell heathers, with the usual two gorse species and specialist flowers like yellow bog asphodel, heath violet, English stonecrop, wild thyme and tormentil. Added to the bright orange of perching stonechat, pink of linnet and subtle green-brown of the meadow pipit, and hopefully the plangent summer cry of the cuckoo and suave dress of the wheatear, this can be a great place on a sunny day. All around, the rugged coast and rolling interior of Anglesey is spread out like a tapestry. Overhead, tumbling common ravens add their own signature, sometimes tussling with yakking peregrines, skirling choughs and chacking jackdaws, or winter flocks of starling, fieldfare and redwing. Check the gulls, too, as the odd Iceland (told by all-white wings) has lingered here.

The other obvious place to look for birds is in and around the small settlement and lake, Cors Fawr (F), rather grandly named the 'big marsh'. Its appropriate F&F includes willows, phragmites reed, soft rush, cotton grass, 'hybridising' horsetails and summer flowering bogbean. The lake is also noted for a rare form of pillwort, a small creeping fern but looking more like a runty grass. Apart from grey heron, a few mallard, 'mere-hen' and coot, little grebe and skulking water rail, the rest of the waterbirds are mainly a motley crew of farm-duck crosses, or opportunistic gulls. Of smaller birds, we should expect reed bunting, swallow, house and sand martin, swift, chiffchaff, willow, sedge and grasshopper warbler in summer, alongside typical resident passerines like pied wagtail, goldfinch, chaffinch, house sparrow, blackbird, the two thrushes, tits, robin, dunnock and wren, sparrowhawk, collared dove, wood pigeon, and other corvids like carrion crow and rook. The shallow lake is fished as it contains rudd, plus introduced roach and even some fearsome pike, and the marshy surrounds hold common frog and toad, plus the widespread palmate newt, at the very least.

Rabbits are the most common mammal, but there is brown hare, hedgehog, mole, red fox, several bat species, and the usual array of shrews, mice and voles so beloved of hovering kestrel and common buzzard, or questing stoat, weasel and polecat. Doubtless otters get up here, too. This is particularly prime adder, slow-worm and common lizard territory, but, as always, they are often secretive, and the many insects much more noticeable. Butterflies, moths, caterpillars, dragonflies, grasshoppers, crickets, ladybirds, bees, hoverflies and lacewings, spiders and

Top : Curlew

Left : Buff-tailed
Bumble Bee

Right : Yellowhammer

NOT TO SCALE

Bottom : Marsh
Marigold

Above: Curlew. *Middle left:* Buff-tailed bumblebee and true lovers knot moth. *Middle right:* Adult male yellowhammer. *Below:* Marsh marigold.

Bog asphodel.

beetles are always the most obvious, but ants, worms, earwigs, pill bugs, and many other indefatigable miniature workers are the unseen heroes of such complex ecosystems. As well as the commoner butterflies, we can see small skipper, small heath, meadow brown, common blue, small copper and gatekeeper; moths like magpie, six-spot burnet, emperor, hummingbird hawk moth; dragonflies and damselflies like emperor, southern hawker, common darter and blue; grasshoppers like common green or mottled; white- and red-tailed bumble and honey bees; crab and jumping spiders; and red and black ants. Yes, just a few of the thousands of insects, with 1,500 different moths alone found on Môn!

As on Holyhead Mountain, there are circular Iron Age earthworks called 'Cwtiau Gwyddelod' (Irishmen's huts), demonstrating some of the many interactions of our busy Celtic past.

SITE 31: THE DINGLE AND AFON CEFN
OS reference SH 453-783, 430-770

SITE 32: LLYN CEFNI
OS reference SH 458-759

It you want a superb little wildlife walk (and a few hours free supermarket parking and shopping) on which dipper, kingfisher and grey wagtail are all possible, even sometimes in the town centre, then try Anglesey's premier market town: Llangefni. Its popular nature reserve, the Dingle, more or less begins in the town by a historic church. With the picturesque Afon Cefni flowing through it, the site now also boasts red squirrel and otter in its little wooded valley, as well as common raven, brown trout, wood mouse, eight bat species, several amphibians and reptiles, many butterflies, insects and wild flowers. It is also part of a very pleasant valley walk up towards Llyn Cefni reservoir. The official entrance is

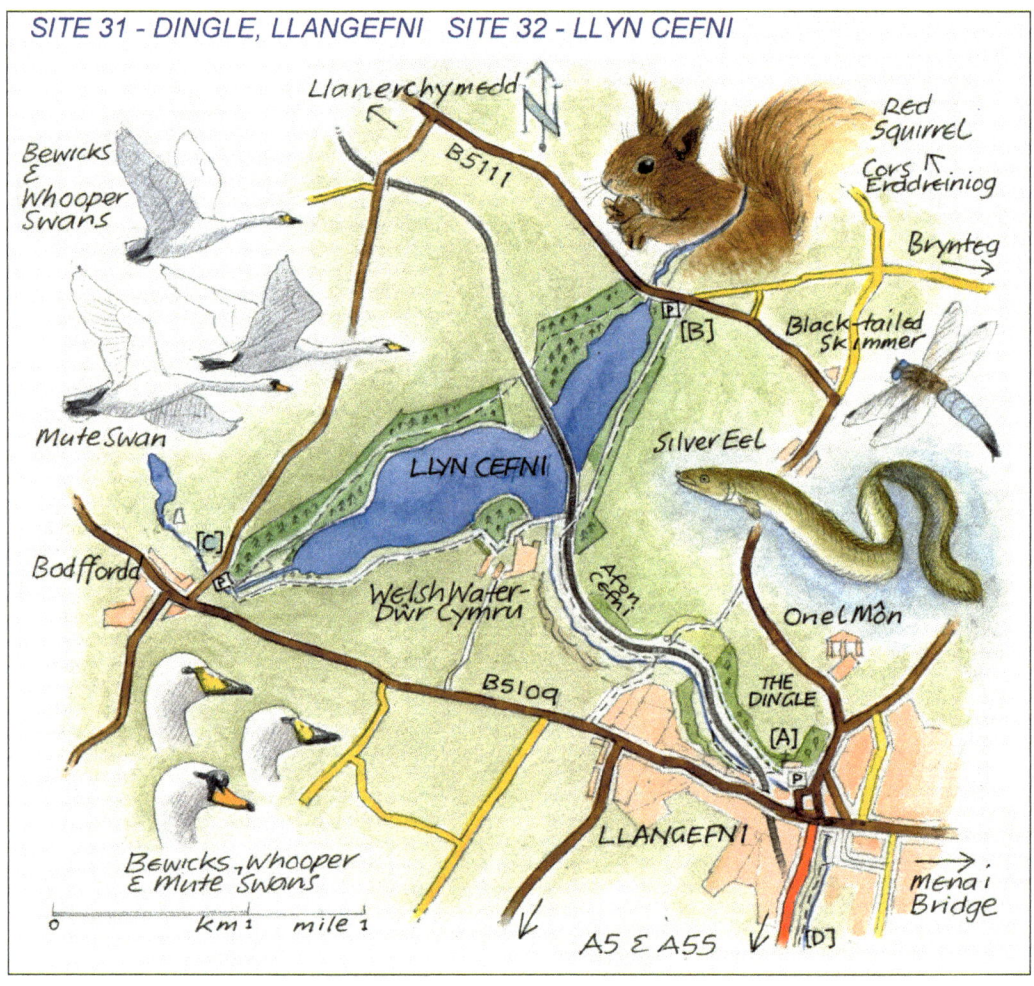

SITE 31 - DINGLE, LLANGEFNI   SITE 32 - LLYN CEFNI

through the large wooden sculptures by St Cyngar's Church and car park, which has a very informative notice board (A).

The Dingle is a LNR (Local Nature Reserve) covering 10 hectares (25 acres) and very rich in wildlife as well as history, as one of its Welsh names indicates – Nant Y Pandy ('Valley of the Fulling/wool-processing Mill'). It also used to supply both the town flour mill and the old railway (that traverses the valley) with water power, as seen in the weir, fish ladder, little lake and water tanks (further upstream). A boardwalk now allows wheelchair and pushchair access right by the river (but no bikes). Nevertheless, the undulating woodland walk nearby is also a cycle track, and soon levels out before leaving the wood and carrying on beside the river up to the reservoir. There is a great bilingual web resource at 'Discovering The Dingle Local Nature Resource', from which some of this info comes, as well as other information boards on site. It's certainly one of most important woodlands on Anglesey, when its rich wildlife, history and geology are taken into account. It has some twenty-four tree species, many over 200 years old, including superb common beech and Scots pine, plus sessile oak, ash, sweet chestnut, sycamore, wild cherry, hazel and crack willow by the river, among several other 'pussy willow' species.

With both dry and wet areas and many slopes, the woodland is an important habitat for many different plants, flowers, ferns, mosses and over 200 fungi species. The flowers include, from early spring, lesser celandine, snowdrop, wood anemone, marsh marigold, primrose and, in places, large swathes of bluebell and wild daffodil, as well as lots of greater woodrush and wood spurge. Unfortunately, they also include Himalayan balsam, a non-native and very invasive plant notoriously difficult to get rid of, although good for some insects.

As for birds, dipper and grey wagtail can be seen on almost any part of the little river (note the footpath and cycle track continue south-west of Llangefni, through the marketplace and another little wooded nant (D), and onto Malltraeth). Likewise grey heron, which like kingfisher, are often seen by the little lake. Other birds include typical woodland species like nuthatch, greater spotted and (sometimes) green woodpecker, tawny owl, jay, and the usual smaller birds, such as tit species including long-tailed tit, finches including bullfinch and siskin, redpoll, robin, wren, dunnock, blackbird, song and mistle thrush. Common ravens and other corvids such as jackdaws love to play on the winds above the trees, along with circling common buzzards and questing sparrowhawks. Down on the river, the slower sections also have nesting 'mere-hen', and sometimes a mixed bag of mallard and ex-farm duck crosses, including Muscovy duck.

With the vale's very 'soggy bottom' the boardwalk traverses, amphibians like common frog and toad and newts like palmate newt naturally abound in season. The omnipresent adder and common lizard prefer the drier and more open parts of the upper woodland, or the rocky slopes of the picturesque upper valley. Dragonflies and damselflies, butterflies and many another insects also naturally thrive. There are many butterfly species, such as the usual speckled wood, orange tip and gatekeeper, as well as moths like vapourer and heart and dart, and many other insects like hoverflies, bees and wasps, beetles, slugs and snails, spiders, woodlice and pill bugs, to name just a few.

For the nature detective, it's both fun and informative to see the difference in the hazelnuts and conifer cones that different mammals nibble on. Red squirrels often

Adult dipper.

just split the nuts lengthways, bank voles (and some birds) tend to leave an irregular hole in the shell, while wood mice leave a neater, more uniform line of little teeth marks around it. As for cones, red squirrels leave little but the stem, while greater spotted woodpeckers leave irregularly projecting scales. Otters don't usually leave much of their fishy prey, but you can sometimes discover bits like fins and tails.

Fish like the brown trout, roach and perch may be seen and fished for in the little lake, Llyn Pwmp, while sea trout and silver eel, as everywhere in Anglesey, are seasonal visitors.

Llyn Cefni is the second largest of Môn's four reservoirs, and its most accessible and utilised – and one of the best for birds. As well as being managed by Dŵr Cymru/Welsh Water, some two-thirds are surrounded by commercial forestry, and the north-eastern half is designated a nature reserve. This is served by a car park and picnic area at (B), on the B5111, forming the end point of a 2.3-kilometre footpath that traverses the whole southern edge of the lake. Passing the spectacular dam, it ends at another parking area by the little village of Bodfodd (C). It is also part of the Lôn Las Cefni Cycleway, up via the charming little Cefni Valley and Dingle. Although the main tracks are mostly well-surfaced, several other paths around the lake are not suitable for wheelchairs or pushchairs, with varying degrees of difficulty.

Coming up from Llangefni gives you the choice of going right or left once at the dam – left to Bodfodd past the fishing hut and pumping station, or right to the official nature reserve end (although sadly no longer endowed with a bird hide and oftimes hard to overlook). Both ends have small rivers entering, thus ensuring shallow, well-vegetated and therefore bird and wildlife-rich areas, thankfully free of boats. Both streams, the Afon Frogwy and Afon Erddreiniog, also host kingfishers especially in the breeding season, when they can be seen – with the usual luck – from either of the two small bridges by the car parks. Note that Anglesey kingfishers often spend non-breeding time on estuaries.

The other notable feature of the reservoir is the track of the Anglesey Central Railway, which used to serve the likes of Amlwch Port to the north, although long out of use. Here it crosses on an embankment, much overgrown with brambles, but used – illegally – as a footpath to halve the circuit of the reservoir.

Naturally, wildfowl dominate the birds at any time of year, but numbers vary accordingly. Some can be both breeding and wintering species, like the attractive diving ducks, common pochard and tufted tuck, or commoner dabbling ducks like mallard, gadwall, shoveller and teal. Of the sawbills and other diving ducks, red-breasted merganser, goosander and goldeneye are regular winter residents, also in varying numbers. The smart smew is sadly a rarer visitor nowadays, while wigeon can winter in good numbers, as can mute swan and coot especially, although both also breed here. Note that scores of whooper swans usually winter in nearby fields so sometimes also found on the lake alongside the mutes, or the usual flocks of non-migratory Canada and greylag geese. As on most Anglesey waters, the beautiful great crested and little grebes both breed and winter, the former often to be seen carrying stripy young on its back, the latter ceaselessly diving for small fish and aquatic insects. 'Mere-hen', skulking water rail, grey heron and regularly visiting great cormorant and shelduck make up the rest of the waterbirds, although the grey wagtails that regularly breed and winter below the dam could also qualify. Dippers, too, sometimes make it this far up the river.

Barn owls are occasionally seen, particularly on the mixed and marshy ground at the top of the Cefni Valley, which is also good for stonechat, winter snipe and woodcock which spend their days hidden away in the trees. Mainly conifers, they naturally attract the more uncommon passerines like red crossbill, siskin and redpoll, while bright bullfinch stand out among the many chaffinch, goldfinch and linnets, with agile long-tailed notable among the three other usual tit species. Among many woodland birds, great spotted woodpecker (plus the odd green), nuthatch, treecreeper, goldcrest, summer warblers like willow, garden, chiffchaff, blackap; with jay, carrion crow, rook, raven, tawny owl and wood pigeon, plus the usual other garden and woodland species, stand out. Firecrest is the usual scarce winter visitor to wooded, insect-rich sites by water, as here at Bodfodd Treatment Works by the car park. With so much watery margin, typical wetland/edge species include year-round reed bunting, or sedge warbler, whitethroat and cuckoo in summer. Ring-necked pheasant and red-legged partridge head up the game birds. Sparrowhawk, kestrel and common buzzard are the main raptors, although red kite, goshawk and, predictably, fish-eating osprey are increasingly dropping in. The fishers could easily breed, should they find a large enough and undisturbed patch in the managed conifers. Peregrines, meanwhile, as elsewhere on Môn, can visit most anytime, especially when the surrounding fields host large flocks of winter waders, like green or golden plovers, or large flocks of starlings whirl around before heading for their various roosts.

In spring, this is one of the first places to see sand martins, sometimes in their hundreds, then varying numbers of swallow, house martin and swift throughout the summer. Many of the waterbirds are here for the fish, of course, and many will be eating the abundant three-spined sticklebacks, as well as any small rudd or perch, or even brown trout, especially stocked for the fishery. Otters, too, for obvious reasons, are taking advantage of such places (sometimes cavorting in the daytime with cubs here), although they often prefer silver eels and even swan mussels and common frogs. Common toads, too, plus the usual newts like palmate, are found, and in drier areas, common lizards, slow-worms and adders can adorn the licheny walls, clearings and rocks.

As for other mammals, the usual island residents here include red fox, polecat, stoat, weasel, brown hare, European rabbit, badger (possibly) and most of the rats, mice, voles and shrews including brown rat, wood mouse, water vole and water shrew. The insect-rich reservoir and woods are also an obvious draw for bats, such as commoner ones like brown long-eared and the two pipistrelles, with the odd noctule, whiskered or Daubenton's also all possible.

Such large watery expanses and margins will have a whole host of insects, particularly flying ones, of which the many *Odonata* (dragon- and damselflies) are among the most striking. Note they also like hunting forest rides or clearings. Môn hosts some fifteen species, the most recognisable being spectacular hawkers like the golden-ringed and emperor dragonflies, darters such as the common/red darter, or the powder blue male or gold female broad-bodied chaser. Black-tailed skimmers, too (which are mainly blue!), are also often found sunbathing on tracks, and among the damselflies, the variable and banded demoiselle damselflies, as well as common blue and blue-tailed, are common enough. Those fishermen's favourites, caddis, stone and mayflies, are also typically widespread in summer, although spending most of their lives underwater as nymphs before their often spectacular hatching as fully-flying imagos. However, it is as nymphs that they are beloved as food by everything from dippers and little grebes to fish, even being eaten by large diving beetles and their own voracious nymphs, or those of the many *Odonata*. Cefni Reservoir undoubtedly has very rich underwater F&F, although I have not yet fully explored it, nor the other insect life apart from obvious butterflies and the like.

Butterflies and moths are also fairly plentiful, consisting of usuals like orange tip, small tortoiseshell, red admiral and peacock, or commoner moths like silver Y and buff-tip. Once again the other insects are far too many to detail, but typically include various bees, grasshoppers, crickets, spiders, harvestman, ants, snails and slugs, plus several ladybird species, and more noticeable beetles like the massive cockchafer, violet ground or bloody-nosed beetles, and various shield bugs.

Although many of the trees are commercial forestry species such as Sitka spruce and pines, there are good numbers of hardwoods like willow, alder, hazel, birch and sycamore. Plants are often dominated by a veritable jungle of brambles, ferns such as royal and hart's tongue, fireweed, large umbellifers like sanicle, ground ivy, mosses and lichens. On the water we find large mats of white water lilies and pink-flowering amphibious bistort, while lesser reed mace and sweet reed-grass fringe much of the lake. Spring and summer flowers include lesser celandine, snowdrop, daffodil, marsh marigold and red campion, with several common fungi like fly agaric, saprotrophic fungi (parasites) like sulphur tufts, or brackets such as peacock-tail and birch-bark polypore.

Far less welcome here is the toxic blue-green algae, or cyanbacteria, which can kill dogs drinking or bathing. Thankfully it is a warm-summer-only phenomena, told by its spreading, almost oil-like, blue-green skeins. Note that some parts of the lake might have restricted access for short periods in the winter shooting season.

LNR, Lôn Las Cefni Cycleway, Welsh Water/Dŵr Cymru.

Violet ground beetle and hawthorn shield bug.

SITE 33: CORS BODEILIO BY TALWRN
OS Reference SH 506-773

Cors Bodeilio (A) is our final limestone fen but smaller and something of a hidden gem, found on a narrow, windy C road between the villages of Pentraeth and Talwrn. It is an NNR, SSSI and SAC due to its rare wetland of alkaline, calcareous fen, plus a small elevated, flower-rich grassland. Although similar to the other fens, it is still 'a unique mire which lies in a shallow limestone valley', with a long ridge overshadowing the north-west. It also owes much to a Wales-wide LIFE Wetland project that curtailed the excessive drainage, the usual evidence of old peat cutting.

The paths don't quite go around all of the reserve yet, but you can extend the walk to Talwrn and back along other interesting undulating tracks and the little wooded C road. Such quiet lanes are rich in birds (such as jay), insects and wild flowers (like wild garlic) in the summer. Paths beyond the site can be very muddy, but, fortunately, an excellent boardwalk from by the parking area and information board (B) stretches for 700 metres around the north-eastern edge of the reserve, before heading off through the little orchid-rich meadows and hedges, although parts can also be rather wet.

Typical wetland plants include some of the rare rushes of other Anglesey fens, like black bog rush, with great fen or saw sedge, cross-leaved heath, and lots of the usual common reed and juncus rushes. White water lilies are one of the flowering water plants that decorate bits of open water, while the slightly drier sections have the parasitic, insectivorous round-leaved sundew and common butterwort. Once again, though, it is the gorgeous if sometimes inconspicuous orchids that attract many. The exotic fly orchid, especially, and narrow-leaved marsh orchid and probably lesser butterfly orchid, although others like the many common spotted and marsh orchid 'crosses' are usually far more widespread. There are more trees here than the

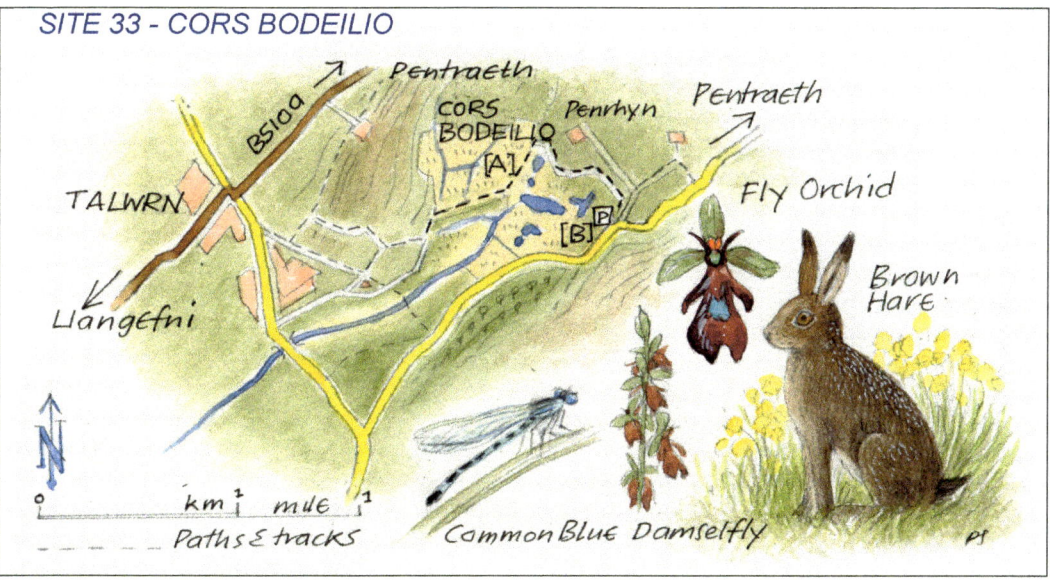

SITE 33 - CORS BODEILIO

other fens, and 'pussy willows', as at Cors Gôch, are several 'pussy willows' species popular for their lovely spring catkins. Hazel and downy birch also have catkins, with another tree, the alder, noted for its little cones beloved of birds like siskin.

Although not particularly noted for fungi, the uncommon little olive earth tongue (*Microglossum viridian*) has been discovered, looking not unlike the black hairy earth tongue of Newborough Forest, or the similar hare's ear – wonderfully weird! The many insects are dominated, at least visually, by the fifteen or so species of dragonflies recorded, many as at previous fens, including several typical hawkers and darters, and the uncommon scarce blue-tailed and variable damselflies. Similarly, the butterflies include the commoner earliest types like orange tip butterfly or small pearl-bordered fritillary, and the possibility of the uncommon marsh fritillary. Medicinal leeches are likewise rare nowadays, but largely due to changing medical fashions. As they mostly prey on amphibians as well as fish, birds and mammals, it is wetland losses that also limit their numbers, plus the usual agrichemicals.

Mammals that rely on water face similar threats, although hopefully water voles, like our otters, are also coming back here, although the voles also depend on the ongoing trapping of American mink. Other mammals such as our beloved brown hares are also doing well enough at Bodeilio, although possibly only if the dreaded and mutated form of rabbit myxomatosis doesn't arrive (it is thought to have jumped to the UK from European brown hares). Red fox, stoat, weasel, polecat, mole, various mice including harvest mouse, voles and shrew species including the water shrew also do well enough given that much of our wildlife is usually under some threat or other. Bats, of course, too, always subject to having their old buildings demolished or renovated, although some still live in hollow trees and can even be seen out on winter afternoons when mild enough. As can the towering smoke-like columns of winter gnats, intent mainly on breeding, not biting.

Common frogs and toads, plus newts, especially palmate, naturally abound in season, which can begin early in the year and therefore be scuppered by frost. Sometimes the evidence is the discarded whitish jelly of frogspawn on the banks, seemingly discarded by grey heron or otter. Of the reptiles, adders and common lizards will probably be the commonest, with the extremely variably coloured snakes able to live in damp or dry heath and mire. As for fish here, we can probably rely only on three-spined stickleback, rudd and the migratory silver eel.

One of the birdy highlights is the lapwing, which are able to both breed and winter here, with its plaintive 'peewit' and extreme aerobatics enlivening at any time

Polecat.

of year. As are lesser numbers of waders like common snipe and redshank, as well as more aquatic birds like 'mere-hen', water rail and little egret. Other avian specialities are the beautiful barn owl and yellowhammer, both endangered and dependent on old-fashioned pasture and farmland methods, like late hay cutting, winter stubbles and flower-rich field margins and headlands. Likewise, birds like reed bunting, grasshopper and sedge warblers, lesser whitethroat or cuckoo all add the distinctive sounds that so define wetlands. Stonechats also need 'unimproved' ground, hence they are found in virtually any open habitat on Môn, from mire to heath to dune.

NNR, SAC, SSI, AONB

SITE 34: MOELFRE

SITE 35: LLIGWY BAY

SITE 36: MARIANGLAS COMMON
OS reference SH 494-873

Moelfre is both a popular little holiday village and a great centre for all manner of interests, from beach and marine to walking, bird and cetacean study, history and archaeology. Its little fishing harbour may mainly host leisure craft nowadays, but the swish RNLI Seawatch Centre, plus new lifeboat station, shows its ongoing importance to shipping. This is certainly seen in its many famous shipwrecks, like the *Royal Charter* of 1859 or even lingering memories of sea battles with Henry II!

The area is also typical of eastern Anglesey's more sheltered and limestone-cliffed coast and sandy bays, small woods, nants and intimate little field systems. Seeing Moelfre from the glorious cliff walk of the Anglesey Coast Path is one way of arriving, from both north or south. Coming up from Red Wharf Bay and Benllech takes you via the busy little beach of Traeth Bychan, but you can see typical coast birds, cetaceans, wild flowers, reptiles like common lizards, butterflies like common blue, insects like tiger beetles, etc., from much of the path. It is especially productive and scenic once past the village and lifeboat station (A), along the Swnt Strait between the headland and little Ynys Moelfre. The most noticeable birds, during any season, will usually be the great cormorants and shags that breed on the isle, with the three regular gulls, great black-backed, herring and lesser black-backed (mainly summer), plus the equally noisy black-headed gull and the odd winter common gull, or a few effortlessly gliding fulmar petrels. The silvery rocks are also home to the vociferous, pied oystercatcher, appropriately dressed to match the summer sea pinks, along with subtler redshank and curlew, or wintering turnstones, and the odd purple sandpiper. Terns like sandwich, Arctic and common often dominate in the summer, plunge-fishing for sand eels and whitebait in the racing green waters of the little strait, or all along the north-west coast, especially up to Dulas Estuary and beyond, where they breed.

Other seabirds found here are mainly summer (although including spring and autumn), like the many northern gannets, Manx shearwaters and auks like razorbills, guillemots and a few black guillemots, as well as increasing numbers of common scoters, throughout the year They are often joined at either end of

SITE 34 - MOELFRE 35 - LLIGWY 36 - MARIANGLAS 37 - AFON DULAS

Amlwch A5025

Llynas Point

Dulas

Curlew ♂

[H]

[F] P

City Dulas

DULAS ESTUARY

Ford

Afon Goch

[G]

Brynrefail

[C] LLIGWY BAY

Mynydd Bodafon

P

[B]

Royal Charter Memorial

Spring Squill, Thrift & White Campion

[D] Din Lligwy

Ynys Moelfre

[A]

Whitethroat

MOELFRE

A5025

Anglesey Coast Path

Paths & tracks

Parciau

[E]

Lesser Octopus

P

Marianglas

Llangefni

0   km   1

mile   1

Benllech

MENAI BRIDGE

PS

Common lizard.

summer by varying numbers of other sea duck, various grebes, divers, skuas, petrels, rarer shearwaters, kittiwakes and the like (see especially Point Lynas (Site 38)). Many of these, however, are either uncommon, sporadic or more deep sea, so red-breasted merganser, black guillemot, red-throated diver and great crested grebe are among the commonest to be seen closer inshore, or parasitic birds like Arctic or great skuas, which energetically harass terns in late summer.

This is fast becoming one of the best places to see cetaceans like common and bottle-nosed dolphins, common/harbour porpoise, and some of the many grey seals that frequent the coast, especially by Ynys Dulas. There are already several boat trips out to see the charismatic mammals, but remember they are regularly seen from the cliffs and are nowadays sometimes accompanied by the large, pale and blunt-nosed Risso's dolphin.

Naturally, the other marine life is equally rich, ranging from chameleon-like lesser octopi to hordes of almost transparent sea gooseberries. In addition to many typical flowers like pyramid orchid, sea pink, yellow kidney vetch, blue squill and white sea campion, the limestone karst 'pavement' clifftop typically host colonies of bright orange *Xanthoria* type lichens or tufty grey-green *Ramalinas*. Below them will usually be typically white-ish lichens, down to the broad black band of *Verrucarias* at the tideline. Beneath that, a silvery barnacle zone is exposed at low water, with many seaweeds from wrack species to the large *Laminaria* kelp forests only exposed at very low tides, or smaller edible treats like traditional Welsh laver bread (*Porphyra* species), similar dulse, and carrageen and bright green sea lettuce. Virtually any rock/shore pools are worth a look, their unique web of F&F ranging from several orangey starfish species to pink encrusting corallina seaweed, beadlet and other anemones, hermit, edible, velvet-swimming and shore crabs, blennies and butterfish to common prawns and shrimps.

All manner of fish are also plentiful enough, if not always easy to catch on rod and line – mackerel and scad are predictably the easiest, from the rocks, when summer shoals come closer in. Sharks will always grab attention, although they are largely dogfish species, now renamed as catsharks hereabouts, with the larger tope and starry smooth hound mainly found offshore, like stingray and common skate. Some of the commoner fish encountered from the rocks are various wrasse species fish already described at sites such as Llanddwyn Isle, like pollack and coalfish, well-camouflaged flatties like plaice and flounder, or the charismatic Atlantic bass. You could see the needle-nosed garfish, too, or other oddities like

Dragonet.

bright sea scorpion and lumpfish, exotic dragonet, or lesser pipefish and especially various jellyfish! Do be careful of the stinging, red-brown lion's mane jellyfish, which have long, near-invisible tentacles, although other common species like moon and compass jellies are 'largely harmless'.

As for terrestrial mammals, you could theoretically encounter many typical Anglesey residents, like brown hare, although otters nowadays get more or less anywhere rivers enter the sea, as at Lligwy (C). Reptiles like common lizard, slow-worm and adder are much more likely, with the usual caveat as to their elusiveness. Heading north from Moelfre on the increasingly undulating Coast Path soon takes you past the Royal Charter Memorial (B) to the popular Lligwy Beach, which has its own little sandy car park, tourist and food outlets. The bay is also of interest to geologists as the place where the silvery Carboniferous limestone met and quarrelled with the underlying red Devonian sandstone, before being enveloped in the Ice Age boulder clay that still causes quicksand problems here. Otherwise, it is the first and largest of two fine sand beaches leading up to Dulas Estuary. Being sandy, these bays are rich in shellfish like razor clams and common cockles, as well as more common winkles and whelks, pretty little tellin species or large otter shells, and many others.

There are several birds possible hereabouts, at various times, including coastal waders like whimbrel, sanderling, ringed plover and common sandpiper, or kestrel, common buzzard, stonechat, whitethroat, meadow and rock pipit, linnet, pied wagtail, chough, jackdaw and common raven. It is also well worth leaving the coast to see several well-preserved archaeological sites, all within a mile or so of each other. There is the very impressive fourth-century Romano-British settlement of Din Lligwy nestled in the trees (D), a Neolithic chambered tomb or cromlech, six Iron Age hut circles and the shell of a twelfth-century chapel with a fine view out over the coast.

Marianglas Common (E) is chiefly noted for lime-loving plants, even on the village green. It has lots of orchids there in the summer, plus common rock rose, and the likes of wild thyme and salad burnet, although normally associated with acid soils. There is also a small woodland – which, with hazel trees, could well have red squirrels – that also contains the uncommon spindle tree, also seemingly testament to a mix of acid and alkaline soils.

LNR, RNLI, ACP, Geo-Môn

SITE 37: AFON DULAS
OS reference SH 477-882

Dulas Estuary is a fine if not quite hidden gem, well worth a visit for birdwatchers in any season. Parking is somewhat restricted and primitive, at (F) by the little Afon Gôch outfall and ford, as is the main muddy and tidal track out to Dulas Bay, but there can be hundreds of birds dotted about the winding estuary or cavorting above the opposite cliff and wooded ridge. Wildfowl and waders prevail, with breeding shelduck, red-breasted merganser, mallard, redshank, oystercatcher, ringed plover, grey heron and little egret, along with regular great cormorant, curlew, peregrine, common buzzard, sparrowhawk, red kite, barn owl, red-legged partridge, common raven, rook, jackdaw, and typical passerines like stonechat, reed bunting, cuckoo. Sedge and grasshopper warbler, whitethroat and lesser whitethroat are found in the surrounding fields, heath and lanes. The nearby Llysdulas woods and copses are also bird-rich if mainly private, and is now famed for the red squirrels that have rapidly spread back to almost every conceivable nook on Anglesey.

The Coast Path, coming up from Lligwy, has fine views of the estuary and bay from the wooded ridge of Coed Y Gall (G), which has its own rich collection of F&F to be discovered. The path then heads up to the main road by the Pilot Boat pub before cutting back to the estuary over wet fields and a ford.

As is often the case on Môn, there can be far more birds in winter than summer, mainly wildfowl and waders, with changing numbers of mute swans, the usual two geese plus brent, and lots of wigeon, teal and mallard, as well as red-breasted merganser, goosander and goldeneye. Waders are often very well represented by large flocks of green and golden plover, varying numbers of curlew, black-tailed and bar-tailed godwit, dunlin, knot, turnstone, snipe and woodcock, the odd grey plover, jack snipe, plus water rail, great crested and little grebes, and the usual predators like merlin, peregrine, red kite and the odd hen harrier or short-eared owl.

The several wooded sections of the Coast Path will have their own typical bird, mammal, insect and plant species, including the likes of tawny owl, red fox,

Dulas.

pipistrelle bat, speckled wood butterfly, assorted bryophytes and hart's tongue fern, fungi, snowdrops and marsh marigold, to name but a few.

Once past the iconic wooden boat wreck, an attractive beach and very Mediterranean-style house and piney headland, we are back on typical Anglesey coastline, but note the Coast Path northwards only cuts inland back at (H) – you cannot bypass Llysdulas Estate from here. This stony and sandy beach holds other typical birds and marine life, as already described at several sites or overspilling from the estuary as the tides wax and wane. You can also see the long, low islets of Ynys Dulas with its distinctive tower – traditionally holding supplies for shipwrecked sailors – from here, although best viewed by binoculars or telescope from a bit further north. It is home to a large colony of grey seals and typical seabirds like great cormorant, waders and gull species.

ACP.

SITE 38: LYNAS POINT AND PORTH EILIAN
OS reference SH 476-930

This prominent lighthouse headland (A) is particularly famed in the birding world for its 'sea-watching' prowess. It can be approached from the south or west by the Coast Path, but otherwise parking is limited or down by the delightful sandy tourist cove of Porth Eilian (B). It is its position as the top-right corner of Môn that makes it so good for passing and migratory seabirds, especially after a typical autumn gale, when lots of birds are straggling back around the coast into the Celtic Sea and wide Atlantic after being blown into Liverpool Bay.

Yet whether in spring, summer or at year's end, there can be plenty of pelagics (deep sea creatures) both avian and mammalian, including the commonest and most numerous birds like northern gannet, Manx shearwater (and the odd sooty, Balearic, great or Cory's), great cormorant and shag. There's also the regular auks including Atlantic puffin and a few little auks in the autumn, and the usual gull species including common gull, kittiwake, and fairly regular little, Mediterranean – even the odd rare Sabine's gull.

In spring, summer and autumn, the Môn coast can also rely on the three usual tern species, plus the odd roseate, little, black or even white-winged black tern – and recently, (rare!) African or American, royal tern. Marauding great and Arctic skuas, as well as fairly regular long-tailed and pomarine skuas, are another autumn phenomena, such as the tiny storm and Leach's petrels fluttering above the waves, or the usual three diver and three grebe species; red-throated and great northern divers, especially, or great crested grebe with only the occasional, rather similar red-necked grebe.

Sea duck, too, can be very common, especially low, straggling strings of the all-black, common scoter with always the chance of a velvet or even American surf scoter among them. Red-breasted mergansers, goldeneye, pied or brown eiders, the delightful long-tailed duck, and occasional scaup make up the rest. A telescope is a distinct asset, and sometimes patience, so finding a sheltered nook to tuck into is advised for sea watching, when not walking the cliffs to see all manner of other F&F. The common or harbour porpoise is fast becoming one of this coast's big attractions, along with the usual three dolphin species, and even the odd minke or fin whale, and certainly

SITE 38 - LLYNAS POINT & PORTH EILIAN

BULL BAY

Amlwch Port

AMLWCH

Pyramidal Orchid

AMLWCH

A5025

Parys Mountain

Rock Samphire

PENYSARN

Menai Bridge

Grey Seal pup

Long-tailed Skua

Arctic Skuas

Pomarine Skua

LYNAS POINT

[A]

Llaneilian

[B]

Porth Eilian

Lions-mane Jellyfish

Mynydd Eilian

TV masts

Dulas

[C]

Ynys Dulas

DULAS ESTUARY

Anglesey Coast Path   Paths & tracks

the ubiquitous grey seal, as back on Ynys Dulas (C). There are many resident birds on and around the cliffs year-round, including fulmar petrel, razorbill, black guillemot, peregrine, kestrel, common buzzard, chough, common raven, jackdaw, skylark, stonechat, linnet, wren, pied wagtail, meadow and rock pipits, and reed bunting, or summer wheatear, cuckoo, and whimbrel. Other waders like oystercatcher, redshank

Leach's and storm petrel.

and curlew, with winter turnstone and purple sandpiper, often adorn the lower rocks and bays, while rarer birdy visitors recently included Dartford warbler and snowy owl. Well, the odd Lapland bunting or black redstart is much more likely.

Naturally, this rocky coast hosts lots of the usual cliff and maritime heath plants, flowers, butterflies, other insects and reptiles, as already mentioned for several sites, like Sites 1 and 22, if minus just a few specialities like silver-studded blue butterfly and spotted rock rose. Note the common blue butterfly and common rock rose are very similar and just as handsome, and that the Coast Path up from Dulas is sometimes rather rudimentary and very up and down.

ACP

SITE 39: AMLWCH PORT

SITE 40: BULL BAY

SITE 41: PARYS MOUNTAIN
OS reference SH 450-934, 426-944, 437-906

Continuing westwards along the Anglesey Coast Path, the next section to Amlwch is generally lower in elevation and mostly better defined, although otherwise typical in its F&F. I remember in the 1980s this was a good area for a diverse number of species from yellowhammer and grey partridge to nightjar and glow-worm, although cannot vouch for any of them nowadays.

Amlwch Port (A) is well worth a visit for many reasons, from its formerly busy and very picturesque harbour to food outlets and Geo-Môn headquarters. Check out the very appropriate and seemingly annual 'Tall Ships' regattas or races that pass here, as well as steam vessels like the Balmoral that give great views of this 'hidden' coast and some of its wildlife.

Heading back to the cliffs necessarily means bypassing the formerly industrialised (chemicals and gas pipeline) headland of Garreg Costog and brings you into Bull Bay (B). With its sentinel 'East Mouse' seabird islet, it is noted for breeding common

SITE 39 - AMLWCH 40 - BULL BAY 42 - PARYS MOUNTAIN

N

Pollack
Coalfish

Porth
Wen
Bull Bay
A5025

BULL BAY
[B]

East
Mouse

Cuckoo Wrasse

CEMAES

Amlwch Port
[A]

AMLWCH

Porth Eilian

Llyn Alaw

Penysarn

Little Gull
(Kittiwake
& Sabine's
← Gull
1st yrs

Harbour/Common
Porpoise & calf

ps

0   km 1   mile 1

[C]
PARYS MT

Red-legged
& Grey
Partridge

↙ B5111
Llanerchymedd

Anglesey Coast Path

House
Martin

Sand
Martin
Swallow

Paths & Tracks

or harbour porpoises, which can fish very close inshore with their attendant young, especially in the swirling green currents by the low western headland. Other cetaceans, too, and all manner of cliff and seabirds like those at Lynas Point (Site 38), including summer fishing terns, gulls, fulmar, razorbill, black and 'ordinary' guillemot and wintering red-throated diver or great crested grebe. The cliff birds typically include kestrel – often a coastal resident here – and peregrine, or chough, common raven and the usual smaller passerines like rock pipit and bright summer wheatear.

Common ravens at play.

Once again, please refer to virtually any of the other cliff sites for typical coastal F&F, like fish, flowers, reptiles, butterflies and other insects, and note the striking lichens that decorate many of the rocks, or the very diverse marine life that still swarms in these clear waters. Recently, extensive swathes of jellies, including the very large barrel jellyfish, have been seen, and small pollack, pouting and coalfish commonly 'hang' in the weed-swaying green currents hard by the rocks.

Just inland from Amlwch is the prominent Parys or 'Copper' Mountain (C), once again decorated with a characteristic mining tower, although nowadays but a shadow of its incredibly busy past as an international source of copper. This has left almost a shell of a mountain above the many polluted lakes and marshes, although colonies of black-headed gulls formerly bred, as still do the likes of common raven, barn owl, red-legged partridge and stonechat, and in winter various wader flocks, starling 'murmuration' and merlin and hen harrier. The typical heathers, gorses and scrub vegetation around the many shallow water bodies also hold all manner of other F&F – with possibly the special liverwort, copperwort, largely associated with copper mining. Please take great care as there are several hidden shafts, tips and quarry faces by the many footpaths.

ACP, Geo-Môn

Site 42: Port Wen

Site 43: Llanbadrig

Site 44: Cemaes Bay
OS reference SH 405-945, 376-947, 374-937

Once past Bull Bay on the Coast Path, the cliffs slowly grow in elevation and wildness again, complete with dizzying clefts and hidden caves, and the superb aerobatics and charismatic cries of the resident red-billed chough and common raven complement them beautifully. Seabird sightings also tend to increase,

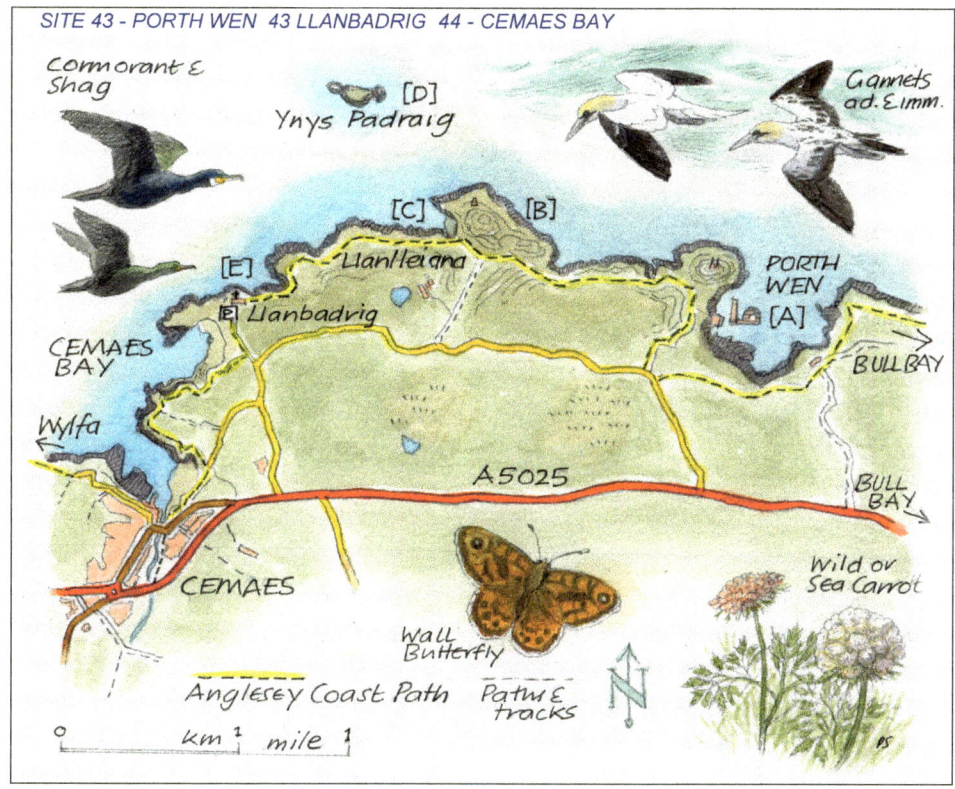

SITE 43 - PORTH WEN 43 LLANBADRIG 44 - CEMAES BAY

Cormorant & Shag

Ynys Padraig [D]

[C] [B]

Gannets ad. & imm.

Llanlleiana

[E]

[E] Llanbadrig

PORTH WEN [A]

CEMAES BAY

BULL BAY

Wylfa

A5025

BULL BAY

CEMAES

Wild or Sea Carrot

Wall Butterfly

N

Anglesey Coast Path   Paths & tracks

km 1   mile 1

especially in summer when lots of terns, gulls, northern gannets, great cormorants, shags, and auks fish or pass to and fro, or skeins of Manx shearwater flash black and white as they skim the rolling waves.

It is from here on that sightings of the massive Risso's dolphin tend to increase, sometimes with the bottle-nosed or common dolphins that have recently interbred with, in the Scottish Hebrides. 'Bottling' grey seals (floating vertically, head up) and harbour porpoises are common, and do look out for 'hurries' of flashing fish fry and sand eels as Atlantic bass and mackerel force them to the surface, sometimes even beaching them en masse in coves and bays. Then there could even be the returning blue-fin tuna or blue shark below them.

Virtually anywhere on Môn's rocky coastline, from Llanddwyn around to Penmon, our hugely varied coast F&F can be seen and studied. From marine life, flowers, bushes and 'scrub', reptiles, butterflies and other insects, mammals, or lichens and mosses to the arty geological melange that underpins it. Distinctive flowers especially stand out, from rock samphire to common scurvy grass, sea carrot to tree mallow, Alexander's to wild cabbage, in addition to the ubiquitous sea pink, blue squill and white bladder campion that decorate the summer cliffs, when not swathed in purple heathers and golden gorses, or gilding bracken.

As elsewhere, butterflies are another great summer draw, so I will only mention small copper and wall here, or the many falls of painted ladies we current enjoy alongside commoner species like peacock. Clouded yellow butterfly is another

Peacock and painted lady butterfly.

increasing southern visitor, as is hummingbird hawkmoth, among many other resident moths like brimstone and white plume, or the many hoverflies, solitary-type wasps or bumble and honey bees – or the very similar but unrelated bee fly.

There are two noted industrial sites on this section of Coast Path, which now becomes very undulating indeed. Firstly, the little stone quay of Porth Wen (A) with its distinctive, igloo-like brick kilns and chimney, then, a mile or so further on, Llanlleiana (C) with its white china clay processing remains. (Note the brickworks are dangerous and no longer open to the public, although many make their slippery way down.) Between them are two superb headlands complete with steep bays, clefts, blade-like rock stacks and the National Trust administered Iron Age hill fort of Dinas Gynfor, though little is to be seen of that (B). That headland is also a SSSI for its geology, as well as having splendid views, sometimes to Cumberland and Man – and, in recent winters, even the Northern Lights.

Peregrines are often hereabouts, although their traditional rock dove prey has long been 'diluted' (in fact they have been strengthened by 'hybrid vigour') with lost racing and feral pigeons, resulting in some particularly particoloured plumages. As the little isle of Ynys Padraig ('Middle Mouse') (D), or is well in view here, the new unfolding phenomena of breeding Môn northern gannets can be enjoyed in summer, if the many auks don't crowd them out again, as they have just done in 2019. Actually, there can be many seabirds here at almost anytime of the year, what with all the fishing terns, gulls, great cormorant and shag, sea duck and other 'passing trade', or gale-bound birds of many types. On the cliffs themselves, the usual (darker) rock and ('greener') meadow pipits demonstrate well their overlapping territories and subtle plumage differences, while stonechat and summer wheatear are also typical, with linnet and whitethroat occupying the scrubbier bits, and, below, oystercatchers going noisily about their business.

Llanbadrig Point and Church (E) is another notable National Trust site, complete with a little car park and convenient clifftop viewpoint and bench. The church was reputedly founded by St Patrick, the shipwrecked Christian missionary, in the fifth century after sheltering in a cave below. The cliffs hereabouts, as well as enjoying many of the other flowers already mentioned, typically have two blooms more associated with woods – bluebell and primrose. Naturally, there are many associated insects, and slow-worms and common lizards are also characteristic, with a whole mass of other F&F overflowing into the many small fields, marshes, rocky heaths and well-hedged lanes just behind the rocky coast. Lesser whitethroat, garden warbler, bullfinch, long-tailed tit – even hopefully the formerly common yellowhammer – wood pigeon, lapwing, snipe, curlew, sparrowhawk and common buzzard can all be seen hereabouts amid the usual garden-woodland birds. With so many little watery habitats, we can also expect the usual amphibians and other aquatic life.

This section of Coast Path finishes at Cemaes Bay, which, with its fine, enclosed beach and little harbour, good selection of shops, eateries and other services including a busy Heritage Centre, is a very popular tourist spot. It also boasts regular sightings of otter, kingfisher, dipper and grey wagtail in its intimate little river valley, 'Nant y Dyfrgi' ('Otter'), just behind the main street.

SSSI, NT, ACP, Geo-Môn

SITE 45: LLYN ALAW
OS reference SH 372-855

Situated just above the old market town of Llanerchymedd, this large Welsh Water and former fishing reservoir has many typical Môn waterfowl, sometimes in good numbers, but unfortunately some of the access suffers from severe neglect. In fact, the north-eastern bird hides and picnic area (B) have long gone and now even the lakeside paths to it are often impassable or overgrown – if you can get through the locked gates on the public footpaths in the first place (as in December 2019). Mind you, one of the main attractions, a breeding common tern and black-headed gullery isle, has also long been abandoned by the terns. Also, the terns mainly fished off nearby Dulas Estuary (Site 37) for marine fish, only occasionally taking the small rudd here, and the reservoir itself, dating from the 1960s, is supposedly not yet a mature ecosystem. Whooper and the odd Bewick's swan still winter in the surrounding fields that enclose this flooded former marsh, called Cors y Bol, although the swans also graze nearer to our other large reservoir, Llyn Cefni (Site 32).

Access then is mainly restricted to the official entrance, car park and dam in the south-west, by Bod Deiniol (A), although that too has lost its visitor and fishing centre. You can also overlook the waters from several points on the little C road to the north-west of the lake, but I cannot always vouch for other footpaths. The margins are well established by lots of waterside plants such as common reed and greater reed mace, white water lily, and narrow strands of trees including several willow species, hawthorn, hazel, mountain ash, sycamore, and assorted conifers. They are often undergrown with the usual hart's tongue and other ferns, or tangles of bramble, bracken and umbellifers and the like, at least assuring nesting places for mallard, geese and possibly common sandpiper and snipe. Winter woodcock, like snipe, prefer the wet margins and soggy field bottoms, and when the lake edges dry out in summer, all manner of other waders can be found, if sometimes only briefly dropping in. These include regular lapwing, golden plover, ruff, greenshank, green, wood and curlew sandpiper, bar and black-tailed godwit, little stint, dunlin, curlew and oystercatcher, as well as the odd black tern. The resident 'mere-hen', coot, water rail and mute swans can nest in or on the edge of the reeds and waterlogged willows, or its several bays. But then the lake covers 777 acres and is around 3 miles long.

The most noticeable birds are usually the hundreds of tufted ducks, great cormorants, greylag and Canada geese, or gulls, mainly herring, black-headed with

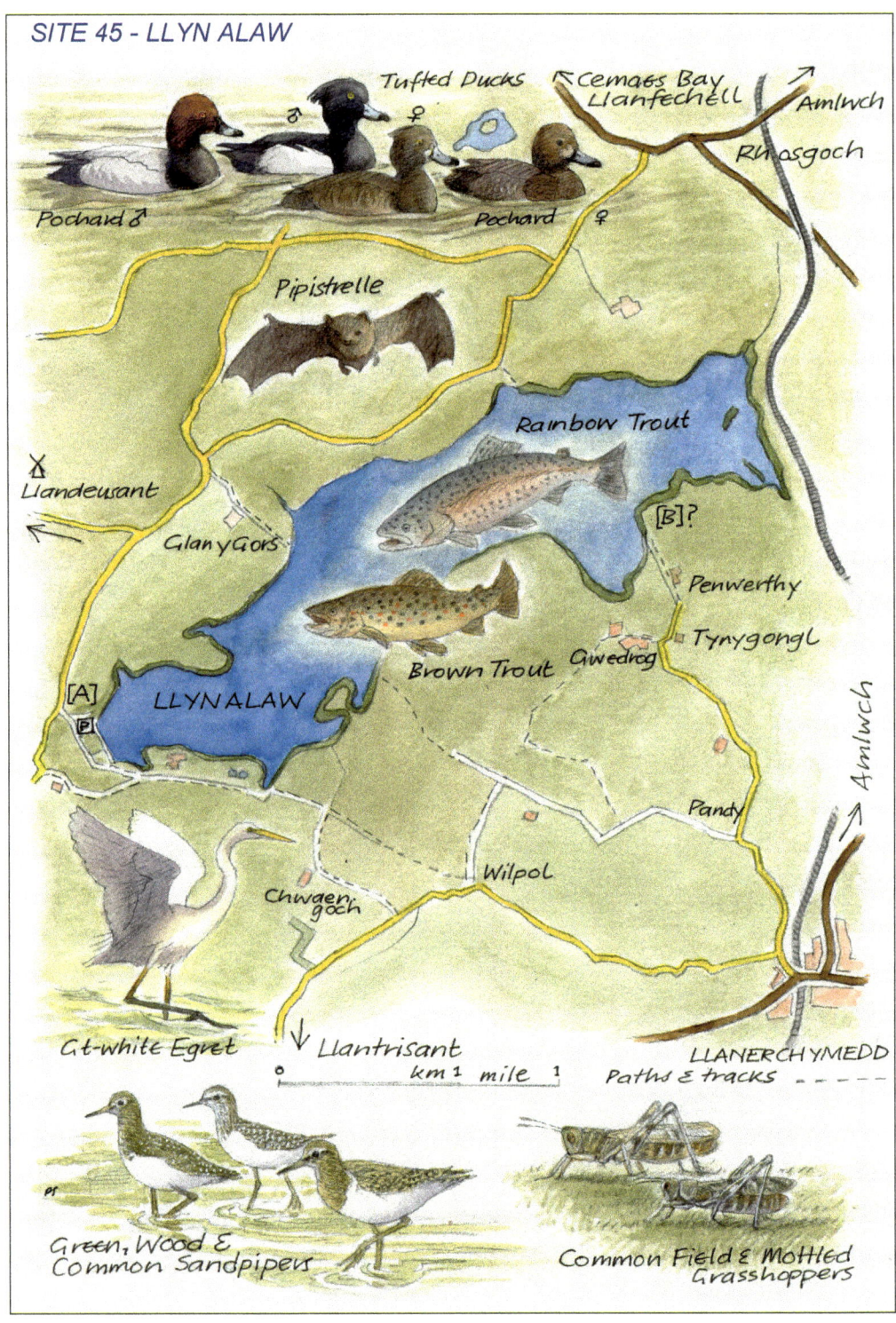

SITE 45 - LLYN ALAW

Tufted Ducks
Cemaes Bay
Llanfechell
Amlwch
Rhosgoch
Pochard ♂
Pochard ♀
Pipistrelle
Rainbow Trout
Llandeusant
GlanyGors
[B] ?
Penwerthy
Tynygongl
Gwedrog
Brown Trout
[A]
LLYN ALAW
Pandy
Amlwch
Wilpol
Chwaen goch
Gt-white Egret
Llantrisant
0   km 1   mile 1
LLANERCHYMEDD
Paths & tracks - - - - -
Green, Wood &
Common Sandpipers
Common Field & Mottled
Grasshoppers

a good few great black-backed, that spend a large part of the year on the water, or at least roost (little gull is also a fairly regular visitor). There have been hundreds of pochard here in the past, but they are generally declining, and now share the winters with goldeneye, diving in the deeper waters along resident great crested and little grebes. Other breeding waterfowl include shoveller and gadwall, joined by teal in winter and shelduck, which are often found inland, even breeding, on Môn. Kingfisher, grey heron and now little and even great white egret fish the margins, while there can be literally hundreds of summering or autumnal gatherings of hirundines like swallow, house and sand martin, and swifts. Around the bushier edges of the lake, especially to the south-west, the likes of whitethroat and lesser whitethroat, or willow, sedge, grasshopper and Cetti's warbler, bullfinch, long-tailed tit, reed bunting, siskin and lesser redpoll can all be seen. The more open and 'unimproved' margins will host stonechat and even summer whinchat, with another decliner, the barn owl. Game birds, as ever, are dominated by the many ring-neck pheasant put down by local shoots, although Grey Partridge were formerly common.

In the winter, the resident geese are sometimes infiltrated by a few pink-footed, barnacle and white-fronted geese, although all have far larger flocks in other parts of Britain. Our most regular winter flocks are of smaller birds like finches (always check for the orange and white flash of brambling) or fieldfare, redwing and starling. They can often be seen flitting from tree to tree in the large areas of open countryside around the lake, which has its trademark narrow lanes, small stone churches and farms – and, nowadays, many large white wind turbines. Kestrel, sparrowhawk and common buzzard are also typical, as well as common raven, carrion crow and jackdaw, wood pigeon and collared dove, and many of the other regular woodland and garden birds where appropriate. In summer our raptors are often joined by the odd hobby, and in winter by equally wandering merlin, red kite, hen harrier and short-eared owl, with peregrines guaranteed virtually anytime, anywhere.

Otter is the most charismatic mammal hereabouts, although they range wherever there is water. Red foxes also like water bodies for the chance of delicacies like duck eggs or chicks, while all the other Môn mammals are possible,

'Backswimmers'.

especially bats like the two pipistrelles, brown long-eared and Daubenton's at dusk, and hopefully water voles – especially if mink have been eradicated here, as hopefully elsewhere on the island.

As for other water life, attractive three-spined sticklebacks (or 'red breasts') live their hectic little lives out in the shallows, along with the usual dragonflies and damselflies and their ferocious larvae or nymphs, or assorted water beetles, water boatman, backswimmers and whirligig beetles, stone, caddis and mayflies, or daphnia, freshwater shrimps and water fleas. Rudd, silver eel, brown and (introduced) rainbow trout eat most of them, and are the only officially recognised fish here, but since Welsh Water's fishery closed some years back, species recording remains uncertain.

The lake has also attracted many avian rarities, ranging from unusual ones like rock thrush to white-winged black tern and, what was formerly uncommon but is no longer, spoonbill.

WW, SSSI

SITE 46: CEMLYN BAY AND LAGOON

SITE 47: WYLFA HEAD NATURE RESERVE

SITE 48: THE SKERRIES
OS reference SH 330-936, 356-938

West of Cemaes Bay the Coast Path continues along low cliffs to Wylfa Local Nature Reserve (A), but as part of the uncertain Wylfa B nuclear power station site, its future is possibly in the balance. It is otherwise an attractive place with the usual cliff maritime heath F&F as well as a woodland nature trail, and boggy areas with characteristic summer stands of yellow flag iris, or wild flower meadow. Plus many of the usual passing seabirds, as covered at nearby Cemlyn. Chough, skylark, stonechat, linnet and the two pipits are among the regular coastal birds here, with water vole among the many small mammals, and you should always expect reptiles like adder, slow-worm and common lizard, and amphibians in such open, damp but also dry rocky habitats.

Cemlyn Lagoon (B) is one of North Wales Wildlife Trust's finest and most-visited reserves, if somewhat man-made and set on National Trust land. It was in the 1930s that Captain Vivian Hewitt acquired the large walled house, Bryn Aber, and set about building the dam and weir by the present western car park (C), forever changing the former saltmarsh into the shallow lagoon we so enjoy today. This was also largely thanks to the unique 'elliptical shingle storm ridge' that encloses the brackish pool and separates it from the sea, also providing a great habitat for several unusual plants. All these propitious circumstances enable water salinity and levels to be maintained to maximum effect for Cemlyn's star attraction – nesting terns. There are usually well more than a thousand terns present in the summer, mainly sandwich, common and Arctic terns, along with black-headed and the odd Mediterranean gull, and all nesting on the lagoon's two little islets. They also protect the birds from most land predators, if not peregrine, grey heron or otter. In fact, as with RSPB's Cors Ddyga and red foxes, low electric fencing was recently employed to keep otters out, and lasers utilised to deter the nightly herons. Note the formerly nesting roseate terns

SITE 46 - CEMLYN 47 - WYLFA HEAD 48 - THE SKERRIES

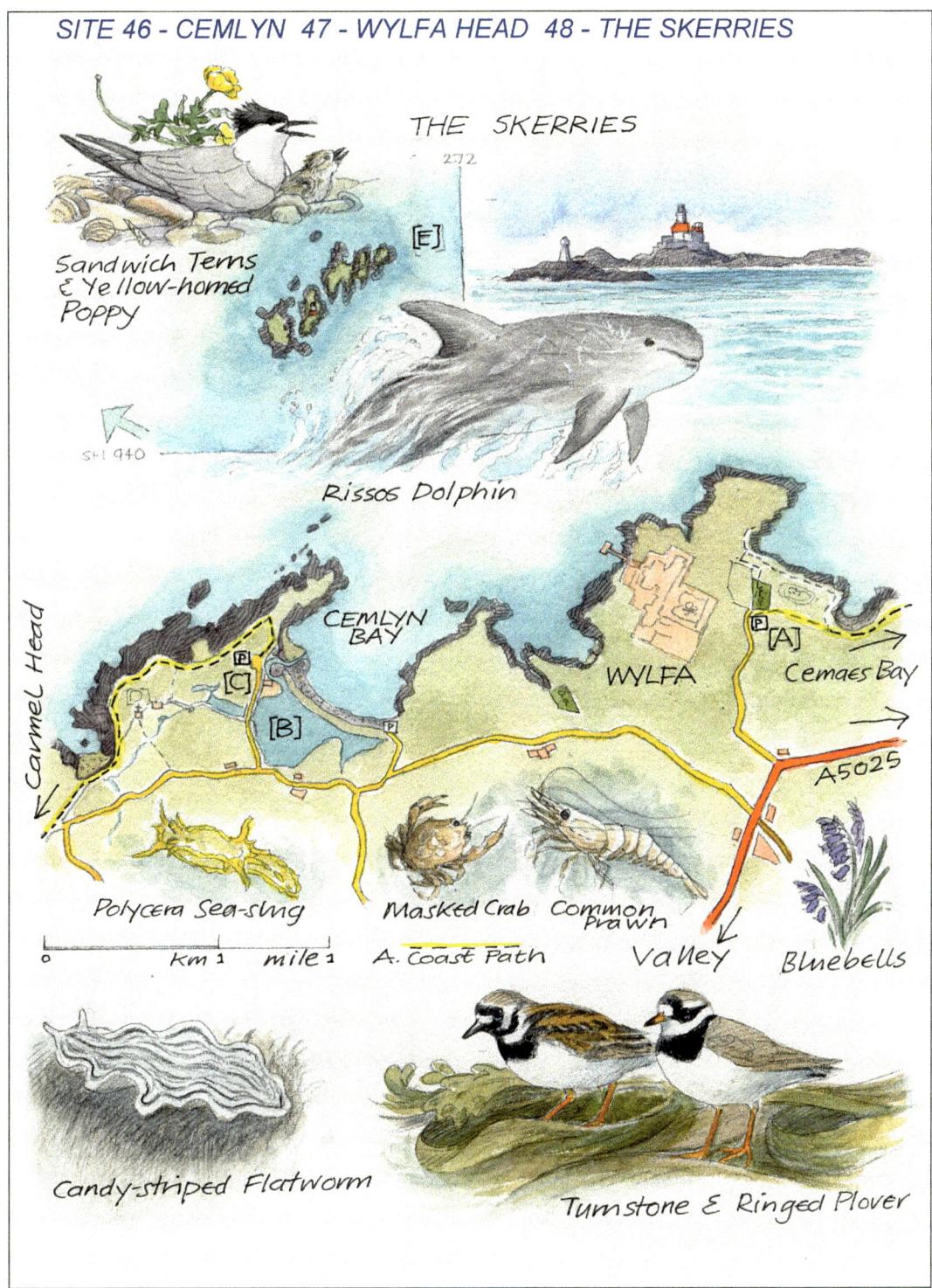

THE SKERRIES

272

[E]

Sandwich Terns & Yellow-horned Poppy

SH 940

Rissos Dolphin

Carmel Head

CEMLYN BAY

[C]

[B]

WYLFA

[A]

Cemaes Bay

A5025

Polycera Sea-slug

Masked Crab

Common Prawn

A. Coast Path

Valley

Bluebells

0   km 1   mile 1

Candy-striped Flatworm

Turnstone & Ringed Plover

have largely skipped over to Ireland, chasing their favourite fish, but odd ones still turn up here, or 'hybridise' with common terns out on the Skerries.

The close proximity of the shingle ridge also means Cemlyn is one of the best tern-watching spots anywhere, with NWWT information and warden usually available – but note the rope barriers, and please keep dogs on a lead. A few other birds like oystercatcher and ringed plover can nest on the ridge, even the odd tern, looking especially scenic among the silvery pebbles, yellow horned poppy, sea kale, sea beet, sea pinks, sea campion and sea purslane. There is the usual rich collection of other coastal habitats, from beach and bay to rocky headland, cliffs and islets, and adjacent farmland. These all provide great habitat for birds, mammals, reptiles, flowers and fungi. Seabirds, waterfowl and waders naturally figure strongly, as well as a huge range of migrant and vagrant birds. On the lagoon, hirundines and swift, kingfisher, mute swan, shelduck, mallard, teal, shoveller, tufted duck, pochard and red-breasted mergansers are regular, or with added wigeon, goldeneye, eider and long-tailed duck in winter. The odd Slavonian grebe, too, either on lagoon or sea, along with the common great crested, red-throated diver, eider and goldeneye, great cormorant and shag. As for other waders, redshank can breed, and make for a good comparison with spotted redshank on passage – unless in spangled black summer splendour. The fields are also noted for flocks of resting 'Northern' Golden Plovers (blacker faces) in spring, or urgent calls of both 'seven whistler' whimbrel and curlew. On the rocky, sea-weedy headland and little sandy indents, grey plover, turnstone, purple sandpiper, dunlin and sanderling are seen mainly in the winter, and common sandpiper in the spring or late summer. The usual stonechat and linnet, meadow and rock pipit, adorn the gorse, heathers and rocky margins around the bay.

Late summer into late autumn is another special time here, what with all the passing northern gannets, Manx and other shearwaters, all four skuas, four grebes, three divers, petrels including Leach's, gulls including little and Sabine's, and sea duck, especially lots of common scoter – sometimes many of them seen in the same session! That's only after a particularly good south-westerly wind though. Cemlyn is particularly well known for a whole raft of rare birds, although as Môn has no breeding ones, yellow wagtails (sometimes blue-headed race) are especially prized, or brighter Greenland wheatear, cuckoo, whinchat, water pipit and Lapland bunting, or

Terns at Cemlyn.

largish flocks of white wagtails. And that's without mentioning black-winged stilts, bridled and Caspian terns, little shearwater, squacco heron, Isabelline and red-backed shrike, shore lark or wryneck, and many more. Back to more normal sights, this is also a good area to see some of Anglesey's diminishing little and barn owls.

One of the commonest lagoon fish is the grey mullet, often seen nosing the surface from March to October when 'inland' for breeding, and thus beloved of hovering ospreys, another regular visitor to Anglesey waters, that must soon nest. As for other marine life, local family the Culley's have found, in addition to low-tide species already mentioned, shanny, black rock goby, five bearded rockling, fifteen-spined stickleback, long broad-clawed porcelain, hairy and Montague's crabs, cushion star, 'Purple Henry' starfish, corkwing wrasse, squat lobster, polycera sea slug and candy-striped flatworm. Just offshore, we have one of the best places to see the large Risso's with the other two dolphins, or harbour porpoise and plentiful grey seals.

Continuing along the Coast Path leads to yet more cliffs, some Ice Age boulder clay, or you can walk on the flat past a side lagoon and marshy fields, leading to one of Môn's oldest churches, Llanrhwydrus (D), through Tyn Llan farm. The path continues westwards to Carmel Head (Site 49).

Brown hare, red fox, rabbit, stoat and weasel are the commonest mammals, and common lizard, slow-worm and adder are the most frequent reptiles, usually best seen when basking on rocks or walls.

With such varied habitat, flowers, plants and insects are here in astronomical numbers, so look for orchids in the boggy areas, where the hugely variable early marsh orchid and spectacular marsh helleborine stand out, with large numbers of pyramid orchids generally in drier areas. The main cliff vegetation will often be bell and cross-leaved heathers, bracken, and a whole mix of flowers, grasses, mosses and lichens

Yes, this is an area hard to beat, especially when looking out from the cliffs over the green or deep blue sea to the beacon of the 'West Mouse' and Skerries lighthouse (E), with grey seal crystal clear in the waters below. Another common growth on grassy clifftops and fields are fungi, with aniseed-smelling horse, and parasol and field mushrooms, and puffballs of varying sizes, all common enough in late summer. That's also when flocks of forty or more choughs acrobatically zoom along the cliffs and add yet another distinctive sound and element to the scene. As do the many butterflies and moths on the blooms, such as common blue, large skipper, wall, gatekeeper, grayling and small copper butterflies, let alone the moths and huge numbers of grasshoppers, bees, spiders, beetles and other insects.

The large assortment of moths particularly thrive because of cliff plants like rock sea spurrey, sea campion, sea plantain and sea thrift, hence the rather rare and elusive little thrift clearwing moth, found only here and a few other sites in western Britain.

SITE 48: THE SKERRIES – YNYSOEDD Y MOELRHONIAID
OS reference SH 268-948
Along with Cemlyn lagoon and Rhosneigr's Ynys Feirig, the Skerries form part of an SPA (Special Protection Area) or the (North) Anglesey Tern Colonies. They are the long low line of isles topped with a distinctive red and white lighthouse that is seen just offshore here, and best noted for hundreds of breeding Arctic and common terns, razorbill, gulls and now most of Môn's Atlantic puffins. Others know them as the 'Isle of Seals', or 'Isle of Rabbits', the latter certainly assisting the birds with

SITE 49 - CARMEL HEAD & YNYS Y FYDLYN

Roseate Tern

ad

Black-headed &
Mediterranean
Gulls, winter
imm.

km   mile

Cemlyn

CARMEL
HEAD

A. Coast Path

Mynachdy

Horse
Mushroom

Llanfairynghornwy

[A]

Ynys y
Fydlyn

Hummingbird
Hawkmoth

Chuch
Bay

Red Fox &
Ring-necked
Pheasant

Cemaes Bay

Llan-
fechell

A5025

Mynydd
MECHELL

[B]

Llyn
Llygerian

Valley

Llyn Alaw

Paths & tracks

Rock
&
Meadow
Pipits

Ynys y Fydlyn

breeding scrapes and burrows by keeping the ranker vegetation down. As these are vital isles for nesting terns, including the odd roseate, and as it is RSPB administered, please note there is no public access, and boats and canoes are required to stand well offshore as the birds can be seen close up at the sea without disturbing them.

NWWT, RSPB, SSSI, SPA, SAC, ANOB, ACP

SITE 49: CARMEL HEAD AND YNYS Y FYDLYN

Although this is typical Anglesey cliff and marine heath habitat, it's particularly spectacular and remote, with the cove, sea arch and island of Ynys y Fydlyn (A), Carmel Head, jagged rocks stacks and views to the Skerries and Holy Island. As usual, the 'big three' cliff birds are chough, common raven and peregrine, while kestrel, fulmar, rock pipit, stonechat and linnet also emblematic, although with nearby conifers and pheasant shoot, there are many other birds, although some of the larger mammals are predictably scarce.

You should find much of Anglesey's characteristic F&F here, plus some wildfowl on the little inland pools and large winter flocks of waders on the wet fields towards Cemlyn. Note that some of the Coast Path out to Carmel Head from (A) is closed in the shooting season (October to February), but there are alternative routes, as shown on the Friends of Anglesey Coast Path website, which has print-out maps and instructions – these are dangerous cliffs!

South from here the Coast Path passes through many different habitats, from Church Bay's fine and colourful cliffs and beach (and eateries!) to the long sandy strands down to the Alaw Estuary (Site 6). Slightly inland, there are two more notable sites: Llyn Llygeirian (B) (SH 349-902), a largish wildfowl and fishing lake, which have the usual dabbling and diving ducks, grebes, mute swans, etc., and is noted for a recent wintering lesser scaup; and Carreglwyd shooting estate by Llanfaethlu (SH 310-873), which has permissive paths, woodland, meadows and a lake, and was part of the red squirrels reintroduction scheme.

NT, ACP, FACP

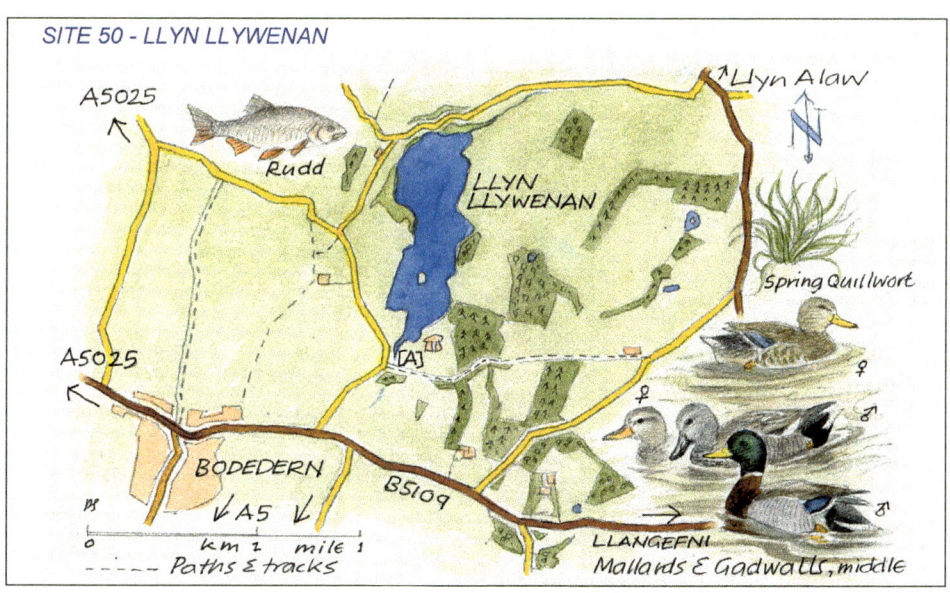

SITE 50 - LLYN LLYWENAN

A5025

Rudd

LLYN LLYWENAN

Llyn Alaw

N

Spring Quillwort

[A]

A5025

BODEDERN

A5

B5109

LLANGEFNI
Mallards & Gadwalls, middle

0   km 1   mile 1
- - - - Paths & tracks

SITE 50: LLYN LLYWENAN
OS reference SH 345-809

This private lake is an SSSI but with few viewing points, either from the northern side road or by the burial chambers at the southern end (A). Its main importance is due to uncommon specialist plants like needle spike rush, eight-stamened waterwort and spring quillwort among the usual rushes and reeds. Amphibians will generally be the same as other Anglesey wetlands, and especially the many aquatic insects in such nutrient-rich shallows, like the usual dragonflies and damselflies and their larvae. There's also lots of wildfowl including breeding mallard, gadwall, shoveller, tufted duck and pochard, the two grebes, both resident geese species, mute swan and great cormorant amid wintering wildfowl such as teal and wigeon. The willow scrub surrounds have typical summer warblers like sedge and willow, alongside resident reed bunting, and many other common birds, or summering hirundines and swift. Marsh harrier, peregrine and bittern are regular visitors, while hobby and freshwater terns are less common. It was formerly home to a black-necked grebe colony, but they have long been only winter visitors, usually on the sea, as at Site 4.

FURTHER INFORMATION

Anglesey Countryside and AONB (Area of Outstanding Natural Beauty) Service

North Wales Wildlife Trust (NWWT), Bangor, Gwynedd

RSPB, Parc Menai, Bangor, Gwynedd

NRW, Maes Y Ffynnon, Bangor, Gwynedd

Cambrian Ornithological Society

Welsh Ornithological Society

Facebook Bird & Wildlife Sightings, Facebook Wildlife of Anglesey

Marine Awareness North Wales (MANW)

Menter Môn

National Trust (NT)

Geo-Môn

FURTHER READING

Hope Jones & Whalley, *Birds of Anglesey* (Menter Môn, 2004)

The Natural History of Anglesey (AAS-Anglesey Antiquarians, 1990)

Snow, P., *Tall Tales from an Estuary* (Coast & Country)

Davies & Roberts, *Best Birdwatching Sites in North Wales* (Buckingham Press)

Williams, Iolo, *Llyfr Natur: Wildlife of Wales* (Carreg Gwalch)

Williams, Iolo, *Llyfr Adar: Cymru ac Ewrop (Birds of Wales & Europe)* (Carreg Gwalch)

Hughes, G. W., *Anglesey at Work* (Amberley Publishing, 2021)

Saunders & Green, *Where to Watch Birds in Wales* (Helm Publishing)

Môn Mam Cymru: The Anglesey Guide (Magma Press)

Whalley, P., *Butterflies of Gwynedd* (First Hydro, 1998)

Conway, J., *Rocks & Landscapes of the Anglesey Coast Footpath* (Geo-Môn)

Hughes, G. W., *Secret Anglesey* (Amberley Publishing, 2019)

BIOGRAPHY

Philip Snow BA is well known for unique bird and wildlife paintings and books, of which this is the eighth he has both written and illustrated. They include the much-lauded *Light & Flight: Hebridean Wildlife & Landscape*; *Tall Tales from an Estuary* and the controversial *Design & Origin of Birds*. He has also provided illustrations or covers for over sixty other books, including Collins Field Guides, many RSPB and other's Reserve signs, limited prints and cards etc. He has also exhibited widely on several continents with paintings in a number of Royal or National Collections, and many private ones. www.snowartandbooks.co.uk